The Origins ... fare
Refo...

STUDIES IN ECONOMIC AND SOCIAL HISTORY

This series, specially commissioned by the Economic History Society, provides a guide to the current interpretations of the key themes of economic and social history in which advances have recently been made or in which there has been significant debate.

Originally launched in 1968 as 'Studies in Economic History', in 1974 the series had its scope extended to include topics in social history, and the new series title 'Studies in Economic and Social History' marked this development. This series was completed in 1995. A new series, published by Cambridge University Press and entitled 'New Studies in Economic and Social History', has now been inaugurated and this includes a number of reissued titles previously published by Macmillan.

Titles still available from Macmillan are given below, followed by a listing of those titles now available from Cambridge University Press.

STUDIES IN ECONOMIC AND SOCIAL HISTORY
(published by Macmillan)

B. W. E. Alford *Depression and Recovery? British Economic Growth, 1918–1939*

M. Anderson *Population Change in North-Western Europe, 1750–1850*

S. D. Chapman *The Cotton Industry in the Industrial Revolution, 2nd edition*

M. E. Falkus *The Industrialisation of Russia, 1700–1914*

J. R. Harris *The British Iron Industry, 1700–1850*

J. Hatcher *Plague, Population and the English Economy, 1348–1530*

J. R. Hay *The Origins of the Liberal Welfare Reforms, 1906–1914*

H. McLeod *Religion and the Working Classes in Nineteenth-Century Britain*

J. D. Marshall *The Old Poor Law, 1795–1834, 2nd edition*

R. J. Morris *Class and Class Consciousness in the Industrial Revolution, 1750–1850*

P . K. O'Brien *The Economic Effects of the American Civil War*

P. L. Payne *British Entrepreneurship in the Nineteenth Century*

G. C. Peden *Keynes, the Treasury and British Economy Policy*

M. E. Rose *The Relief of Poverty, 1834–1914*

S. B. Paul *The Myth of the Great Depression, 1873–1896, 2nd edition*

J. Thirsk *England's Agricultural Regions and Agrarian History 1500–1750*

J. R. Ward *Poverty and Progress in the Caribbean, 1800–1960*

The Origins of the Liberal Welfare Reforms 1906–1914

Prepared for
The Economic History Society by

J. R. HAY

palgrave

First edition 1975
Reprinted 1977, 1980, 1982
Revised edition 1983
Reprinted 1986, 1987

Published by
PALGRAVE
Houndmills, Basingstoke, Hampshire RG21 6XS and
175 Fifth Avenue, New York, N. Y. 10010
Companies and representatives throughout the world

PALGRAVE is the new global academic imprint of
St. Martin's Press LLC Scholarly and Reference Division and
Palgrave Publishers Ltd (formerly Macmillan Press Ltd).

ISBN 0–333–36000–1

This book is printed on paper suitable for recycling and
made from fully managed and sustained forest sources.

A catalogue record for this book is available
from the British Library.

Transferred to digital print on demand 2002
Printed & bound in Great Britain by
Antony Rowe Ltd, Chippenham and Eastbourne

Contents

Acknowledgements

I wish to thank my colleagues in the Departments of Economic History at the Universities of East Anglia and Glasgow and Dr M. E. Rose of the University of Manchester for their comments on various drafts of this book. My debt to the General Editor of this series, for his assistance which went far beyond the duties laid on him, cannot be adequately expressed here.

Notes on References

References in the text within square brackets relate to the Bibliography, followed by the date of publication and, where appropriate, by the page number in italics, e.g. [Briggs, 1961*b*, *222*]. Other references in the text, numbered consecutively, relate to sources itemised in the References section.

Editor's Preface

SO long as the study of economic and social history was confined to a small group at a few universities, its literature was not prolific and its few specialists had no great problem in keeping abreast of the work of their colleagues. Even in the 1930s there were only two journals devoted exclusively to economic history and none at all to social history. But the high quality of the work of the economic historians during the inter-war period and the post-war growth in the study of the social sciences sparked off an immense expansion in the study of economic history after the Second World War. There was a great expansion of research and many new journals were launched, some specialising in branches of the subject like transport, business or agricultural history. Most significantly, economic history began to be studied as an aspect of history in its own right in schools. As a consequence, the examining boards began to offer papers in economic history in all levels, while textbooks specifically designed for the school market began to be published. As a specialised discipline, social history is an even more recent arrival in the academic curriculum. Like economic history, it, too, is rapidly generating a range of specialist publications. The importance of much of the recent work in this field and its close relationship with economic history have therefore prompted the Economic History Society to extend the scope of this series – formerly confined to economic history – to embrace themes in social history.

For those engaged in research and writing this period of rapid expansion of studies has been an exciting, if rather breathless one. For the larger numbers, however, labouring in the outfield of the schools and colleges of further education, the excitement of the explosion of research has been tempered by frustration arising from its vast quantity and, frequently, its controversial character. Nor, it must be admitted, has the ability or willingness of the academic historians to generalise and summarise marched in step with their enthusiasm for research.

The greatest problems of interpretation and generalisation have tended to gather round a handful of principal themes in economic and social history. It is, indeed, a tribute to the sound sense of economic and social historians that they have continued to dedicate their energies, however inconclusively, to the solution of these key problems. The results of this activity, however, much of it stored away in a wide range of academic journals, have tended to remain inaccessible to many of those currently interested in the subject. Recognising the need for guidance through the burgeoning and confusing literature that has grown around these basic topics, the Economic History Society hopes in this series of short books to offer some help to students and teachers. The books are intended to serve as guides to current interpretations in major fields of economic and social history in which important advances have recently been made, or in which there has recently been some significant debate. Each book aims to survey recent work, to indicate the full scope of the particular problem as it has been opened up by recent scholarship, and to draw such conclusions as seem warranted, given the present state of knowledge and understanding. The authors will often be at pains to point out where, in their view, because of a lack of information or inadequate research, they believe it is premature to attempt to draw firm conclusions. While authors will not hesitate to review recent and older work critically, the books are not intended to serve as vehicles for their own specialist views : the aim is to provide a balanced summary rather than an exposition of the author's own viewpoint. Each book will include a descriptive bibliography.

In this way the series aims to give all those interested in economic and social history at a serious level access to recent scholarship in some major fields. Above all, the aim is to help the reader to draw his own conclusions, and to guide him in the selection of further reading as a means to this end, rather than to present him with a set of pre-packaged conclusions.

M. W. FLINN AND T. C. SMOUT

University of Edinburgh *Editors*

1 Introduction

IN the history of social policy in Britain, the years between 1906 and 1914 stand out as one of the periods of major reform. Old age pensions, insurance against ill-health and unemployment, school meals, and medical services for children were introduced. Minimum wages were fixed in certain industries, and some attempt was made to alter the distribution of income and wealth in British society. Ever since, historians have been trying to explain why there should have been such a concentrated burst of activity by the Liberal governments of those years – activity which seemed to run counter to the *laissez-faire* individualist ideology of the nineteenth-century Liberal Party.

Some have treated this as a problem in the history of ideas, seeking to explain why attitudes to social reform changed in the latter part of the nineteenth century [Mowat, 1969; Emy, 1973]. Others have concentrated on the political pressures which forced or encouraged politicians to embark on social reform [Marwick, 1967; K. D. Brown, 1971*b*]. Yet others have examined the underlying economic and social changes out of which the reforms emerged [Phelps Brown, 1959; Semmel, 1960], while a few have concerned themselves primarily with the institutional influences which modified the reforms in the process of legislation [Davidson, 1972]. Each group of historians is interested in the origins of the Liberal reforms though their accounts are inevitably partial, and only a few rash spirits have tried to present a comprehensive account [Halévy, 1932; Gilbert, 1966]. The problem of the origins of the Liberal reforms remains unsolved.

Any satisfactory explanation must put the Liberal reforms into a wider context. Many historians have seen the Liberal reforms as the origins of the Welfare State. The Welfare State, however, is an ambiguous concept, with different implications in different

11

societies. Some historians draw a distinction between a 'welfare state', in which services are provided at optimum standards for the whole population, and a 'social service state', in which minimum standards are provided for the poor [Briggs, 1961*b*, *222*]. The Liberal state was much nearer to a social service state than a welfare state, and the minimum standards were not universally available before 1914 [Read, 1972, *189*].* Old age pensions and national insurance were confined to those who had incomes below certain levels, and both excluded some of the poorer groups.

Social reform has often been regarded as being entirely progressive. It has been treated as the legislative result of a deeper appreciation of social problems, such as unemployment, ill-health, old age and an altruistic desire on the part of governments to help the weaker members of the community. But social reform has, historically, fulfilled other purposes. 'Welfare can serve different masters', wrote Titmuss. 'A multitude of sins can be committed in its appealing name. It can be used as a form of social control. It can be used as an instrument of economic growth which, by benefiting a minority, indirectly promotes greater inequality.'[1] Social reforms have also been wrung from reluctant governments by pressure from political parties, trade unions or other organisations.

Historically the Welfare State is a product of industrial society, for it is concerned, very largely, with the social casualties associated with industrialisation. The ideology of a Welfare State, however, runs counter to that of a capitalist industrial society in many ways, since a welfare state emphasises the narrowing of differentials in society and presupposed interference with the working of labour, capital and, even, product markets. Nevertheless welfare policy can be used, and has been used, to ensure the continued existence of capitalist industrial society through such modifications to its main features.

The Liberal 'social service' state had similar roots. In it a limited range of services was provided for the poor in money and kind. This marked a considerable step forward, since they had

* Apart from this instance the terms 'social reform' and 'welfare reform' have been used interchangeably in this work.

either not been available before, or had been available only under very degrading conditions. But the Liberal reforms were also designed to make the minimum possible alterations in the working of the British economy, to ensure its survival at a time when it was subject to internal and external pressure. It is, nevertheless, true that much of the legislation introduced was capable of extension in ways which would have made fundamental changes in the British economy and society [Harris, 1972, *364–5*; Fraser, 1973, *156–7*].

The origins of social reforms are always complex. Few of the reforms of the period from 1906 to 1914 can be regarded as the outcome of a single set of influences. Not surprisingly explanations of the origins of social reform have been diverse. Nevertheless, they can be fitted into two broad categories. There is, first, the perspective of the social scientist concerned with the reasons for the introduction of social welfare services in different societies. Then there is the historical study of the specific changes in a single society. There is obviously some overlap between these two approaches. Historians often use comparative material, while social scientists err if they ignore the historical context of legislation in individual countries.

The main features of these approaches are outlined in the next section. These different approaches agree on certain common influences, which must in consequence be regarded as important in analysing the origins of social reform. The central section examines these in the light of recent research. The final part looks at the individual reforms, trying to identify, as far as is possible in this intractable area, the particular influences which were important in each case.

2 Approaches to the Reforms

SOCIAL welfare legislation is a common feature of industrial societies, though interpretations of its role in such societies vary [Rimlinger, 1971]. A study of its origins seems to require a comparative investigation of a range of societies. Comparisons may be made with reference to the same period in time, or to societies at the same level of economic development. The theoretical, conceptual and statistical problems involved are enormous, and many regard such attempts as premature and necessarily unsatisfactory, because they can only be carried out at a high level of generality [Martin, 1972, *18*]. Such studies may also tend to ignore or undervalue those differences between countries which are not easily quantifiable.

But comparative studies are necessary. After all, societies as diverse as Germany, the United States of America, Tsarist and later Soviet Russia, Australia and Uruguay were embarking on social legislation, which contained many similar elements to the Liberal reforms, at roughly the same time. Moreover foreign influences were extremely important in the origin of these reforms. Historians usually cite Lloyd George's famous journey to Germany in 1908, out of which came his ideas for national insurance. But surveys of foreign practices preceded most major legislation. Individuals and pressure groups drew heavily on foreign experience as, for example, did Sir Charles Dilke in his plans to curb 'sweating'. The New Zealand Act of 1898 was an inspiration to the National Committee of Organised Labour on Old Age Pensions. The Association of British Chambers of Commerce wanted the Royal Commission on the Poor Laws to examine the whole Bismarckian social insurance network with a view to its adaptation to British conditions, two years before Lloyd

15

George was converted. Examples could be multiplied indefinitely, but the main point is clear enough. What was happening in Britain between 1906 and 1914 was not unique, though its precise form and the motives for specific measures often were. Explanations of the origins of modern social welfare policy in Britain cannot be totally at variance with those applicable to other countries, except in so far as the social context of the reforms in Britain was indeed different.

Economists have shown that the level of social services expenditure, defined as the expenditure by the state on social security, education, health, and welfare services, is positively related to the level of Gross National Product [Pryor, 1968, *150*]. In other words, high-income countries spend more on welfare than low-income ones. The interesting point is, however, that when a sample consisting only of high-income countries is taken, this relationship breaks down [ibid. *474*]. This is, on the whole, what might be expected from late nineteenth-century experience, for it was not Britain or the United States of America which led the way in the provision of social welfare services, but Germany and some of Britain's overseas dominions. A statistical correlation, however, does not, by itself, prove a causal connection, or show which way such a connection runs, and the various historical hypotheses which have been offered to link economic development and welfare require separate examination. Woodard, for example, has suggested that modern welfare legislation was only introduced when a redistribution of income within society was necessary to guarantee levels of consumption sufficient to meet the increased production of industrial societies. This occurred, he argued, in Britain during the Great Depression of the late nineteenth century and in America between the wars [Woodard, 1962].

Demographic and economic explanations may be linked. Rimlinger noted that technological change raised the level of labour productivity in advanced societies, and labour became scarce as population growth slowed down. Therefore, he suggested, governments would find it valuable, on economic grounds, to introduce welfare services which contributed to the efficiency of the worker. Health services would ensure that the worker was returned to the labour force as soon as possible after illness. More generally, by raising the standard of health of the community, especially among children, such services would yield an economic return outweighing their cost. Education would have similar results. Furthermore, using a Keynesian argument, he suggested that unemployment benefits would help to maintain levels of consumption during an economic depression, and act as a built-in stabiliser. Such benefits would also help to prevent the physical deterioration of the worker during periods of unemployment, with the same effects on average productivity as mentioned above [Rimlinger, 1966]. All this seems rather abstract, and far removed from the language of political and economic debate in the nineteenth century, but there is much in common with the principles underlying the campaign for 'national efficiency' which flourished around the turn of the century.

The links between war and welfare have been examined by several writers. Peacock and Wiseman erected an elaborate hypothesis about the effects of war on government expenditure, including that on social services. They argued that, in peacetime, people desire increased spending on social and other services, but they object to the taxation necessary to pay for it. It takes a major catastrophe, such as war, to disturb people's ideas of what is a tolerable level of taxation. During wars, higher tax levels are imposed and borne. After the war, the tolerable level of taxation is higher and governments can now embark on welfare and other projects. Not only that, but wars tend to result in the transfer of responsibility for expenditure from local authorities to central governments, and in the discovery of social evils such as ill health, malnutrition or inequalities in the distribution of income or wealth. Thus, the agenda for state action is increased [Peacock and Wiseman, 1967].

Titmuss, who wrote the excellent official history of the development of social policy in Britain during the Second World War, generalised his conclusions in a brief, but important, article in 1955 [Titmuss, 1963, 75–87]. Drawing on the work of the Polish sociologist, Andrzejwewski, which suggested that inequalities between classes would be narrowed according to the degree to which these classes participated in war, Titmuss argued that,

17

during wars, it was necessary to ensure solidarity on national rather than class lines. This required better social provision and a narrowing of inequalities in society. In addition, some blueprint of a better society as a result of war was vital. Improved social conditions became part of the nation's war aims. Some, though not all, of these effects are identifiable in the case of the Boer War, though they do not occur in quite the mechanistic fashion which these theories suggest.

The problem with such analyses of the effects of war is to differentiate those features which are the result of the war alone, from those which stem from underlying and long-term changes in society. Statistical results do not give unqualified support to Peacock and Wiseman's hypothesis [Pryor, 1968, 444-6]. Social historians have, none the less, stressed the importance of the Boer War in the origin of the Liberal reforms, and it provides a test case for some of the points made here.

Other writers have stressed political influences.[2] Some have tried to construct models of political behaviour which would account for the growth of social services, but without great success [Culyer, 1973, 76-84, provides a convenient introduction]. Among empirical studies of political influences, the most interesting is Pryor's, which concludes that the only variable significantly related to the origin of social welfare schemes is the extent of trade union organisation in a country. As he admits, however, the degree of unionisation and social welfare schemes may be related to some common cause, such as the extent of political interest among the working class. Many historians have argued that the social welfare reforms in Britain were the inevitable result of the extension of political democracy in the nineteenth century, though recent writers have tended to question this simple view.

Marxist writers provided an alternative framework for analysing the growth of welfare services. Welfare reforms are seen as a product of the class structure of society; concessions won from a reluctant state, representing the bourgeoisie, by working-class action. Such 'concessions' can be interpreted in two ways. They can be regarded as 'palliatives' – interim steps in the transformation of capitalist society. Or they can be considered as measures

18

which strengthen capitalist society, perhaps by drawing the workers away from socialism, which thus make revolutionary change even more remote. This difference of interpretation among Marxist historians reflects contemporary debate, among socialists and other radicals at the turn of the century.[3] The Fabians, for example, looked forward to a peaceful transformation of capitalism through collective action, including welfare reforms. Other socialists were extremely concerned that welfare reforms would, in fact, prevent the true interests of the workers being achieved.

There is, therefore, a wide range of general comparative approaches, each throwing light on different aspects of the welfare reforms and putting them in the context of a common response among industrialised societies. Though open to criticism for their generality, they act as an antidote to the very parochial framework, which has marred some historical writing on the origins of the Liberal reforms.

(ii) HISTORIANS AND THE LIBERAL REFORMS

The precise influence of common factors can only be determined by a study of the particular society concerned, and the second category of writing on the Liberal reforms is concerned with the changes in Britain, in the latter half of the nineteenth century, out of which the reforms emerged. To understand the present debate, it is best to approach this aspect chronologically, because historians have been trying to account for the Liberal welfare reforms since they were introduced. Indeed, two of the first historians, the Webbs, were themselves actively involved in the political debates accompanying the legislation [Webb, 1948]. This helped to lend colour and immediacy to their writing, together with a bias which later writers have sought to amend [MacBriar, 1962]. Other largely autobiographical works from this period are still valuable, particularly for the origin of old age pensions.[4]

When the major statesmen of the Liberal period produced their memoirs, however, they tended to concentrate on the background to the First World War and, on the whole, they said little

19

about the welfare reforms. In some cases, this might be explained by a distaste for the politics of the people, or a genuine lack of involvement in the process of reform, much of which was carried through by a very small group of Liberals around Lloyd George and Churchill. It was left to the great French historian, Halévy, to provide what is still the best comprehensive account of the origins of the Liberal reforms in the epilogue to his classic study of Victorian Britain. He argued that Imperialism and social reform were linked responses to the growing conviction that Britain's rate of progress was declining relative to other countries.

Until after the Second World War there were few works of stature, apart from Halévy's, dealing with the origins of the Liberal reforms. Gilbert Slater did range over most aspects of social welfare. Some of his suggestions as to why attitudes to children and the health of the nation changed in the late nineteenth century are of wider applicability. He mentioned the growth of scientific sociology; the strengthening of democracy in political and industrial life; the rise of feminism; the rise in status of medical experts; the fact that children were more highly valued as the birth rate fell; and the shock to complacency brought about by the Boer War [Slater, 1930].

There were, in addition, a few historians of individual Acts and programmes,[5] and some civil servants, who had been involved with the early stages of legislation, published memoirs which threw a little light on the origins of the welfare reforms.[6] These detailed studies were complemented by Helen M. Lynd's work on the 1880s, which dealt with the changing climate of opinion in these years [Lynd, 1945]. Lynd was not the first American historian to bring the freshness of an outsider's vision to the examination of the background of the welfare reforms, and the next thirty years were to see many of her compatriots involved in research in this field. Many of them were concerned to demonstrate the lessons which the United States could learn from British experience, and their work has to be read from this point of view, but they all escaped a parochial approach [Semmel, 1960; Gilbert, 1966].

After the Second World War, when the Labour governments of 1945 to 1951 carried out their programme of welfare legislation, which built on the Beveridge Report and the Butler

Education Act of 1944, and the term 'Welfare State' began to be used, it was understandable that historians should seek to trace connections with the previous period of reform under the Liberals. The Liberal reforms tended to be interpreted as the first major steps on the way to the Welfare State. The Welfare State itself, under the influence of stage theories of economic development becoming popular at the time, was often regarded as a definite stage in the development of capitalist society, and the welfare reforms of 1906–14 began to assume an aura of inevitability. The close connections between the two periods, in the persons of Beveridge and Churchill, lent credence to this view. What Titmuss was to castigate as 'the placid, conventional romance of the rise of the Welfare State' began to appear.

Almost at once the view that the Liberal reforms were a stage in the inevitable progress of British society began to be questioned. There was a reaction against the 'Welfare State' as it existed, or was believed to exist, in Britain in the 1950s. From the right came criticism of the universality of provision and complaints about the rising cost of welfare. The left pointed to the deficiencies in coverage and treatment, and showed that poverty, at least in relative terms, had not been eliminated. With the realisation that the Welfare State in Britain in the 1950s was not ideal came a much more open-minded approach to the Liberal reforms. If poverty and inequality had not disappeared in Britain in the mid-twentieth century, and could persist despite universal suffrage, it was much less plausible to argue that the Liberal welfare reforms were the inevitable result of the limited franchise extensions of the nineteenth century.

Other reasons for the revival of critical interest in the origins of the welfare reforms included the publication of the memoirs of leading civil servants, which now drew attention to the struggles behind the scenes between politicians, civil servants and pressure groups [Beveridge, 1953; Bunbury, 1957]. It became clear that accounts which concentrated on the public and parliamentary aspects of reforms were seriously deficient. The operation of the fifty-year rule, later reduced to thirty, allowed access to the government papers of the period; the papers of major statesmen gradually became available for study as well.

Quite independently of these developments there was growing interest in the relationship between the Civil Service and Parliament as a result of MacDonagh's studies of the growth of government earlier in the nineteenth century. Several historians turned their attention to the Victorian origins of the Liberal reforms.[7] They tended to substitute a new type of determinism for the old, by arguing that the extension of the role of government was the product of a bureaucratic process, in which 'experts' in the Civil Service were the prime movers in legislation rather than politicians.

Meanwhile what used to be called constitutional history was itself undergoing a revolution. Sociology, psephology, and political science combined to throw new light on elections, constituency and central organisation, and the popular basis of party politics. This development cast doubt on widely held assumptions about the inevitable decline of the Liberal Party and its replacement by an independent Labour Party as the franchise was extended. The older view owed much to Dangerfield's brilliant picture of England on the eve of the First World War, but it was supported by more recent work on London and Wales [Thompson, 1967; Gregory, 1968]. Now it was argued that the Liberals had, in fact, adjusted to the new class politics, and that there was no warrant for assuming that a social reformist Labour Party would inevitably replace a Liberal Party which had itself embarked on social reform. Furthermore the evidence from Lancashire seemed to show that on the eve of war the Liberal Party was in good heart; it made more sense to concentrate on the 'progressive alliance' between Liberals and Labour than on differences between them [Clarke, 1971]. Not everyone was convinced by the reinterpretation, and it has been pointed out that the term 'progressive' tended to be used more by Liberals, because it reflected peculiar Liberal values, than by Labour [Petter, 1973]. Also, the growing grass-roots support for an independent Labour Party was contrasted with the alliance between Liberal and Labour politicians, while the growing strength of the Labour Party organisation was demonstrated [McKibbin, 1970]. The debate between those who argue that the Liberal Party was doomed by   and those who stress its continued vitality is necessarily inconclusive, if only because there is no way of removing the First World War from the historical context in the manner of the devotees of counter-factual history. But the debate has implications for the origins of the Liberal reforms. The view which is taken of the character of the British electorate will determine the weight which is given to popular pressure in those origins.

One other type of historical writing which has become very popular in recent years might best be described as the micro-political study of particular social reforms. Studies of this type reveal much about the timing and the shaping of social reform, but since in the blow-by-blow tactical battle it is often extremely difficult to detect the underlying reasons for social reform, some writers have produced what is at most a partial explanation. The conclusions of these studies should always be related to the wider issues raised by social reform in industrial societies. Good recent examples of work of this genre include Macleod's studies of legislation to prevent the exploitation of workers and their families on Britain's canals and of the stunted development of the Medical Department of the Local Government Board.[8] They show how a study of bureaucratic processes can illuminate the history of social legislation at times when public opinion and outside pressures were relatively uninfluential. There is also a neat little debate over the reasons for the appointment of the Royal Commission on the Poor Laws in 1905 which does raise more general problems.[9]

Historical studies thus tend to confirm the importance of political pressures and changing attitudes to social reform. They also suggest that institutional influences should not be neglected. The next section examines these three aspects in turn. Economic developments are not treated in isolation, but are linked to the changing views on the need for social reform.

3 The Roots of the Reforms

(i) PRESSURE FROM BELOW

THERE is a wide measure of agreement among historians and social scientists that political pressure from the working class was one of the main reasons for the origins of social reform. Politicians introduced social reform either to attract electoral popularity or to prevent workers turning to extreme labour, socialist or syndicalist solutions. The latter part of this explanation seems to fit Bismarckian Germany, but both elements have been applied to Britain. T. H. Marshall, for example, traced a progression from civil to political and then to social rights in which he emphasised both popular demand and what he called the 'class abatement' aspects [Marshall, 1963]. Contemporary writers, like Sidney Webb, also saw collectivism as 'the economic obverse of democracy'. As he said, 'if you allow the tramway conductor to vote he will not forever be satisfied with exercising that vote over such matters as the appointment of the Ambassador to Paris . . . but . . . he will . . . seek . . . to . . . obtain some kind of control as a voter over the conditions under which he lives' [quoted in Gilbert, 1966, 25–6].

But there are some problems with simple versions of this link between political democracy and social reform. Why, if social reform was so popular, was it never a major election issue?* Gilbert's answer is that the two major parties were aware that they could get involved in an auction on social reform and made a tacit bargain not to compete [Gilbert, 1966, 449]. Though there is, of course, no evidence of such a pact, the desire for it may well have existed. Senior Liberals deplored 'the political fashion which

* Russell [1973] shows that backbench Liberals, labour and socialist groups did make social reform an issue in 1906, even if the leadership of the major parties was reticent.

has been in vogue that is equally injurious to both parties or the State, of presenting to the country ... not a policy but a catalogue' [Matthew, 1973, *126–7*]. They wished to present the Liberal Party as a party of the nation and to prevent, as was happening on the Continent, a polarisation between socialism and reaction.

But even allowing for Liberal skills in disguising the issues involved, serious problems remain. The time-lag between the extension of the franchise in 1867 and the Liberal legislation is difficult to explain on this hypothesis. Gilbert and others stress the effects of the franchise changes of the 1880s, but these made little difference to either the extent or the effectiveness of working-class pressure.[10] Finally, those who argue that working-class pressure for social reform and income redistribution was strong and effective must take account of the continuing poverty and inequality of income distribution in Britain today.

One simple way out of the difficulty is to deny that social reform was popular and insistently demanded by the working class. Pelling has suggested that 'the extension of the power of the state at the beginning of this century, which is generally regarded as having laid the foundations of the Welfare State, was by no means welcomed by members of the working class, was indeed undertaken over the critical hostility of many of them, perhaps most of them'. He attributes this hostility to the dislike of existing state institutions, especially the Poor Law, but also of state education and local authority 'housing plans'. Trade union support for the Labour Party was given not for social reform and extensions of the role of the state, but for strictly limited aims, such as reversing legal decisions which restricted the activities of the unions, especially the Taff Vale decision. In this the trade unions reflected, according to Pelling, the view of the mass of the British workers [Pelling, 1969, chap. 1].

These arguments have not been generally accepted [Clarke, 1971, *399*]. Hobsbawm feels that Pelling's hypothesis might apply to the 'ordinary, unskilled, uneducated and unorganised masses', but that it is misleading if applied to the organised labour movement. Other historians, drawing on the work of British sociologists, emphasise the importance of deference and the acceptance of some middle-class norms by important sections within the working class, especially those who had been granted the franchise. The working-class voter was not interested in a massive redistribution of income, but expressed preference for only limited social changes which were quite within the compass of the traditional parties. Social reform was only one element which determined voting patterns, and demand for reform was neither insistent nor profound. Moreover support for reform was diffused among competing groups and their influence was thus reduced. Though politics were conducted on a class basis in the late nineteenth and early twentieth centuries, the major parties were not forced into social reform by massive popular demand or fear of revolution, but were able to introduce specific policies to gain a tactical advantage over other parties. Given the character of the electorate, there would be a gradual trend towards social reform, no more. This approach, which is tending to become the new orthodoxy, is closely bound up with the view that the Liberal Party had established a viable base in the new class politics before the First World War [Clarke, 1971, 1972; Emy, 1973, xi].

Here then are three views about popular attitudes to social reform. First, the working class 'as a whole' did not want reform; second, the organised working class did but the unorganised did not; and, third, while there was a demand for social reform, it was limited in scope and quite within the power of traditional parties to provide it. As far as the organised working class is concerned, Hobsbawm is surely correct. Both the Labour Party and the Trades Union Congress had extensive social reform programmes by the early 1900s, including free education for all, asssisted by scholarships; old age pensions; the abolition of the Poor Law; and measures to deal with unemployment. The Labour Party also wanted a comprehensive health service, at the best medical standards, for all, not just a service for the poor [Roberts, 1958, 206; Marwick, 1967]. In this they were looking forward to an 'optimum' rather than a 'minimum' standard, something usually thought of as characteristic of the post-1945 Welfare State [Briggs, 1961b, 224, 228]. Moreover it is very doubtful how far these measures on unemployment, health and education were based on the acceptance of middle-class values. To traditionalists in the major Edwardian parties they were indistinguishable from socialism.

The views of the rank and file of working-class organisations and of the unorganised masses beyond have not been seriously studied, and as a result important questions cannot be answered. Were the ruling élite correct to fear the ultimate presentation of revolutionary demands if social reform was not introduced? What were the attitudes of the poor to social reform? While it may be extremely difficult to create 'a language of the voiceless', as Hobsbawm has requested, the effort needs to be made. Even if Clarke's interpretation of the views of the working-class electorate is correct, it is very doubtful if it would apply to the 40 per cent of adult males who did not have the vote. Studies of the poor in modern Britain and other societies show that their acceptance of the dominant ideology in society is less than total.[11]

Research into popular attitudes can be based in part on existing sources. The local records of trade unions, trades councils, and the working-class press will yield more about the attitudes of rank-and-file workers than has been produced so far, while the work being done in oral history has opened up a new field of evidence on popular attitudes outside organised bodies. It is sad to reflect that more is known about the motives of eighteenth-century crowds and rioters and 'criminals' than about their post-industrial successors. It is time that the activities and motives of these groups were studied, for they did not necessarily represent a throw-back to pre-industrial forms simply because an organised labour movement now existed.

Though firm conclusions are premature it is clear that there was a range of popular attitudes. Some opposed welfare reforms on theoretical grounds, arguing that the economic and political system had to be changed first. Others made a distinction between social and economic reforms. 'To the poor, economic reform means a measure of justice between the "haves" and the "have-nots"; but social reform means "police", whether they are really required or not.'[12] Some had no objection to reform in principle and supported or opposed specific Liberal measures. Finally, there were some who benefited personally from social legislation. The number of working-class activists who ended their days in the new bureaucracy created by the Liberals had implications for the subsequent development of the labour movement [Halévy, 1961 ed., vol. 6, *446-9*].

There remains the problem of the effectiveness of working-class pressure for reform. Some historians see the Labour Party as an appendage of the radical wing of the Liberals which exerted relatively little independent pressure for social reform [Rowland, 1968, *71*]. Others, like K. D. Brown [1971*b*], have argued that it played an important part in the origins of Liberal legislation, particularly that relating to unemployment. There is similarly no consensus as to the influence of popular demonstrations and pressure out-of-doors. K. D. Brown [1971*a*] attributes the Chamberlain circular of 1886, the Unemployed Workmen Act of 1905 and the rekindling of interest in unemployment after 1907 to socialist-inspired popular action [see also Stedman Jones, 1971]. Harris [1972], from a different perspective, rather plays down the influence of popular disturbances, seeing them more as a problem of public order.

In the light of this discussion it is implausible, any longer, to assert that the social reform of the period from 1906 to 1914 was simply the inevitable result of working-class pressure, through the ballot box, or by direct action or the threat of it. This does not mean that such pressures were not important, or non-existent, as some historians have tended to suggest. Rather their influence has to be examined in each case, not brought in as a *deus ex machina* to explain reform. To the extent that working-class pressures cease to be sufficient explanation, it is necessary to turn to the other reasons why the ruling classes of late Victorian Britain changed their attitude to social reform. Why did they decide that social reform was desirable or necessary? In their calculations, working-class attitudes and pressures were only one element, though it was sometimes the most important.

(ii) CHANGING ATTITUDES TO WELFARE PROVISION

The changing attitude to social reform among the political élite was influenced by developments in the British economy in the late

29

nineteenth century. The slower growth of the British economy, its relative decline in industrial production compared with Germany and the United States, and the effects of the 'Great Depression' on profits and prices, had a profound effect on the political classes of Britain. Many influential contemporary figures were conscious of depression and relative decline, but they could not be sure that this would not turn into absolute decline, and it was in this uncertain situation that they began to seek remedies.[13] It has been pointed out that it is at such times that ideologies become conservative, and it is no coincidence that many in Britain turned to Germany, where social reform had been used in an explicitly conservative manner, for the model for key elements in British social legislation.

Earlier writers linked political, economic and ideological pressures and the subsequent development of welfare legislation and extensions of empire in the phenomenon of social imperialism. The idea derives from Marx and was developed by Schumpeter, and their differing analyses influenced the work of Halévy and Semmel. Halévy, obsessed by what he saw as the decadence of late Victorian Britain – the loss of confidence by her governments expressed in the search for alliances in Europe and the extension of the Empire, the decline of individualism and the rise of socialism – found it easy to explain welfare legislation as part of a general search for security by the ruling classes. Semmel distinguished two varieties of social imperialism. The first 'emphasised the need to maintain the empire and . . . asserted that the welfare of the working class depended on imperial strength'. The second started from the condition of the working class, and suggested that it would be impossible to defend the empire without a healthy base. Chamberlain and the tariff reformers tended to take the first line, while Liberal imperialists followed the second. Semmel could see in social imperialism some of the ingredients of fascism, but argued that it was modified by the liberal values of the British party system [Semmel, 1960, 246].

Recent writers, on the whole, have tended to eschew the term 'social imperialism' and concentrate only on aspects of the phenomenon, such as the campaign for national efficiency

[Gilbert, 1966; Searle, 1971]. Concern for the efficiency of the British economy was not entirely novel. Lyon Playfair had predicted in the 1860s what the consequences of the neglect of technical education and physical efficiency would be. But from the 1890s onwards it seems clear that concern in Britain went deeper than before. It was reinforced by empirical studies by Booth and Rowntree and by revelations about the health of army recruits during the Boer War. The war itself, in a wider sense, was the great crisis which brought these latent doubts and feelings of insecurity to the surface [Searle, 1971, *34*]. Concern cut across party lines and, for a brief period, some of the more optimistic devotees of national efficiency looked for a realignment in British politics, perhaps even a separate party, which was to be led by the former Liberal Prime Minister, Lord Rosebery. For some participants the emphasis in the campaign was purely military, but the economic and social implications were linked by Sidney Webb and by Asquith. Webb argued that a national minimum standard of life was essential to national efficiency and imperial strength. Asquith made a similar point when he asked, 'What is the use of talking about Empire if here, at its very centre, there is always to be found a mass of people, stunted in education, a prey of intemperance, huddled and congested beyond the possibility of realising in any true sense either social or domestic life?' [quoted in Gilbert, 1966, *77*].

The practical influence of the idea of national efficiency is difficult to estimate. It certainly helped to give social reform the status of a respectable political issue, and it can be linked directly with two of the· earliest Liberal reforms. But the Webbs, by backing Rosebery against Campbell-Bannerman, reduced their chances of directly influencing the first Liberal administration. However, men who had been involved in the campaign, like Haldane and Asquith, became members of the Cabinet, though they were subject to other influences and their support for particular measures cannot be attributed solely to considerations of efficiency.

Nevertheless the idea of national efficiency became part of the political language of the time, and many found it reasonable to express their support for social measures in such terms. Even a

31

radical Liberal, Sydney Buxton, Churchill's successor at the Board of Trade, was accused of trying to sell national insurance as a 'business proposition'. Certainly there were businessmen in the Liberal Party, and outside it, who supported welfare measures, particularly educational ones, on the grounds that they would contribute to the efficiency of the workers [Harris, 1972, *218*]. Lloyd George arranged for the opinions of German employers on the Bismarckian insurance schemes to be collected, and published selections which stressed the economic advantages. Even before this, in 1906, Birmingham Chamber of Commerce had called for a complete Bismarckian social insurance scheme, including old age pensions. There is evidence here to support Rimlinger's contention that 'the development of modern health and welfare programmes is at least in part a response to the rising productivity and increasing scarcity of labour in the course of economic development' [Rimlinger, 1966]. Education, health and welfare services seemed to promise to become more 'profitable' to the state, as threats to its economic position increased. Economic and political arguments converged. Rimlinger concluded that there was little evidence to support his views, but he had not looked at the literature on national efficiency in Britain.

Not all influential Liberals accepted the analysis of the national efficiency school. Some argued that there was no crisis at all, and took comfort in the evidence of the continuing expansion of the British economy. They also noted that social problems, of no less severity, coincided with high rates of growth in countries overseas. Protective tariffs did not appear to have removed these problems. This was a reassurance when Chamberlain suggested tariff reform as a remedy for some of Britain's economic ills, and as a means of financing social reform. But those who said there was no crisis, like the future Liberal Prime Minister, Sir Henry Campbell-Bannerman, found it difficult to avoid being trapped into the admission that, despite the growth of the British economy, some 30 per cent of the population were living in poverty. It was hardly enough to argue that things were just as bad as elsewhere, or that they might well be worse under an altered system in Britain. Very reluctantly, therefore, they turned to the consideration of possible alternatives. Right up to the eve of the 1906 election, Campbell-Bannerman strove to avoid committing the Liberal Party to any measures to deal with unemployment, or even old age pensions, which had been under discussion since the late 1880s.

If the campaign for national efficiency made social reform a respectable political issue, there were other reasons why ruling-class opinion became more receptive to state intervention [Gilbert, 1966, 60]. One of these was a change in attitudes about poverty. This is often presented, following the Webbs, as a change from a moral to an economic or environmental explanation of the causes of poverty [Woodard, 1962]. Beatrice Webb gave as the reason for this change, the 'class consciousness of sin' among men of intellect and property, as they realised that the growth of the British economy had failed to produce a 'decent livelihood and tolerable conditions for a majority of the inhabitants of Great Britain' [Webb, 1926, 206].

Recent research has tended to modify this picture by showing that much was known about poverty, and some of its economic causes, through the work of Henry Mayhew and a host of Victorian middle-class organisations, before the 1880s [Thompson and Yeo, 1971; Harris, 1972, 1–3, 42, 362; Rose, 1972, 20–33]. MacGregor prefers to talk about 'an organic process in capitalist society', fostered by the desire of the middle classes to preserve existing institutions, and reflected in their growing ability to measure and define 'the economic costs of social wastage inherent in unregulated industrialism'. The need to measure, define and remedy was intensified, from the 1870s, by the social imperatives of an extended franchise and challenges to Britain's economic position [MacGregor, 1957].

The social surveys of Booth, Rowntree and others were important in changing attitudes, but their effects were quite complex. (Their direct influence on reform through more accurate statistical knowledge has been questioned [Harris, 1972, 362; Martin, 1972, 13].) The social surveys did tend to undermine the view that personal character deficiencies were the primary cause of poverty. But Booth's sociology was an uneasy mixture of economic and moral categories [J. Brown, 1968, 1971]. His work helped to confirm widely-held views that the

33

working class could be divided into various strata. There were the skilled artisans and trade unionists, who had been enfranchised in 1867. Then there were the respectable poor, who struggled to maintain a precarious existence independent of the Poor Law. Finally, there was the residuum of casual workers, loafers and unemployables. One great fear among social reformers and politicians was that the respectable poor would be infected by contact with the residuum during periods of social distress, and as a result moral and physical degeneration would set in. Even worse the respectable poor might be tempted to throw in their lot with socialist agitators and elements among the residuum in a struggle for the redistribution of wealth. The riots in London in 1886 and 1887 seemed to show such fears were not groundless [Stedman Jones, 1971, chap. 16].

Many confirmed individualists, therefore, came to see the need for social measures to provide for the respectable poor, separate from the hated Poor Law. Such measures would allow a much harder line to be taken with members of the residuum, who were regarded as being beyond hope. Recent historians have pointed out that the rise of an economic and environmental approach to poverty resulted in a harsher attitude to many of the poor. Such an approach was not confined to the Fabians and to devotees of national efficiency : Marshall was prepared for physical control of recalcitrant parents who did not provide suitable education for their children, and his pupil, Pigou, talked of 'forcible detention of the wreckage of society, or the adoption of some other means to prevent them propagating their species' [Stedman Jones, 1971, *331–6*; Harris, 1972, *42–7*].

Liberal individualists, of course, would not accept such extreme solutions, but late Victorian and Edwardian social legislation is thoroughly permeated by the desire to provide decent treatment and social incentives to the respectable, and to separate them from the residuum.* This was the intention of Chamberlain's circular of 1886 and the Unemployed Workmen Act of 1905 [Harris, 1972, *76, 161*]. Even old age pensions, as introduced in 1908,

* Marshall wanted artisans to be associated with the operation of Poor Relief, because he believed they would take a stricter line than middle-class guardians. *Official Papers* (1926) p. 210.

were not given to the habitually improvident or the pauper, and workers who were dismissed for misconduct lost their right to unemployment benefit under the National Insurance Act of 1911 [ibid. *314*]. Each of these measures was designed to benefit the respectable poor, to incorporate them into society and to strengthen their resistance to the blandishments of socialism. As A. J. Balfour put it, 'social legislation . . . is not merely to be distinguished from socialist legislation but it is its most direct opposite and its most effective antidote' [quoted in Fraser, 1973, *129*]. This opinion was to be echoed by Lloyd George and Churchill in the Liberal era.

The final aspect of the change in opinion is often referred to as the rise of collectivism [Pinker, 1971, *85–92*]. What happened between 1860 and 1900, however, was more a shift of emphasis as to what constituted legitimate collective activity rather than a revolution in thought. Historians agree that the Oxford philosophers, T. H. Green and D. G. Ritchie, contributed largely to this shift. Green's idealism, in its political implications, was far from being a collectivist philosophy, but it accepted a more positive role for the state in a basically individualist society [Emy, 1973, *6*]. Ritchie argued, against both Mill and Herbert Spencer, that the relationship between the state and the individual was an organic one. 'The state and the individual are not sides of an antithesis between which we must choose' [quoted in Bullock and Shock, 1956, *189*]. These ideas were taken up by a younger generation of intellectuals, who were very influential in the councils of the Liberal Party in the twentieth century. J. A. Hobson agreed on the need to recognise the 'organic relation in the growth of human wants'. Consequently it was necessary to satisfy the lower material need as a precondition for the moral improvement of man. This view was shared by Asquith, Lloyd George and many other Liberals. C. F. G. Masterman called for the redistribution of income as a prime social need. 'If anything is wrong in material conditions, it is in the apparatus, not of accumulation but of distribution' [Masterman, 1909, 1960 ed., *162*].

The New Liberalism, then, was not an abandonment of individualism, but a reinterpretation. This distinction is a fine one, but to contemporaries it was very real. According to several

35

recent writers, the idea of social justice 'provided the means of reconciling individualism and collectivism', and allowed a radical reinterpretation of Liberalism [Mowat, 1969, 93–4]. Social justice required that each privilege and institution was not absolute but relative to the wider welfare of society. This ideal provided a guide through practical debate and an answer to 'any determinist (individual or collectivist) attempt to realise ultimately similar goals through the impersonal working of industrial and economic forces'. Such a reinterpretation was absolutely necessary because Liberalism faced, for the first time, the challenge of an alternative radical philosophy – socialism.

This is not the place to analyse the true content of the revived socialism of the late nineteenth and early twentieth centuries. Socialism at this time was the great bogey, and Liberals alternated between fear and contempt for socialism as a doctrine. They feared its implications for the type of society they wished to preserve or create. They feared the consequences of their own failure to create that society, a socially responsible form of capitalism. They had little but contempt for what they regarded as socialism's over-simplification of economic and social processes and its nebulous utopianism. Liberals felt that socialism would result in the primacy of sectional interests, instead of a society where interests were balanced for the common good. So Liberals, even the most radical, were concerned to discriminate between their ideas of state action to liberate the faculties of the individual, and what they saw as the complete control of economic and social processes by the state.

The Liberal response to socialism took various forms. It was often argued that socialism was not a practical philosophy but rather a vague utopianism. There was some contemporary warrant for this, at least till around 1890, in the published work of leading British socialists. But, from the 1890s onwards, the Independent Labour Party and the Social Democratic Federation set out political programmes with very specific reforms attached, such as the eight-hour day, and the right to work. These were intended only as palliatives, pending the reconstruction of society with collective ownership of the means of production. To this, the Liberal reply was that such proposals were impractical precisely because they would undermine the basis of capitalist society. Socialist programmes did, however, present measures which advanced Liberals could adopt, provided they were modified to reconcile them with Liberal philosophy.

Another common Liberal response to socialism was to attempt to incorporate the philosophy within the British political tradition. This went hand-in-hand with practical steps to incorporate working-class leaders into the political establishment. Socialism was redefined as a vaguely progressive spirit, coupled with whatever practical steps the Liberals were taking at the time. Thus Harcourt and Morley could both claim that, in all practical and beneficial aspects, Liberalism encompassed socialism. But this was a double-edged sword if, in practice, there was little apparent difference between the Liberal legislation and the palliatives of the socialists. It was all very well for an economist like Marshall to say that 'a cautious move towards enriching the poor at the expense of the rich seems to me not to cease to be beneficial, merely because socialists say it is a step in their direction'; but Liberal politicians were very sensitive to the charge that they were the 'tools of the socialists'.

Socialism, of course, was not a unified philosophy in Britain before 1914. There were several differing varieties including the 'Marxism' of Hyndman and the Social Democratic Federation and the Fabianism of the Webbs. The older historiography, powerfully influenced by the Fabians, tended to stress the contribution made by them to the origins of the Liberal reforms, but most recent studies have swung to the other extreme. MacBriar concludes that, 'no major political development can be attributed with certainty to Fabian influence: but few similar groups, so small and so much outside the established centres of power, can have exercised as great and as varied an influence in minor but not unimportant ways' [MacBriar, 1962, 349]. Any reassessment of Fabian influence must start with a sociological analysis of the membership of the Fabian society, dominated as it was by the emerging middle-class professional groups of late Victorian England. It has been argued that the failure of these groups to establish a place in the social structure of Britain conditioned the failure of the Fabians to influence political development, though other historians still argue that any failure was the result of tactical errors [Hobsbawm, 1964, chap. 14].

(iii) INSTITUTIONAL INFLUENCES

In recent years some institutional pressures and counter-pressures which influenced the welfare reforms have been brought to light. Pressure groups, civil servants, and representatives of existing institutions, including the local authorities and the Poor Law, modified the proposals for reform in various ways. Earlier historians virtually ignored pressure groups in studying the origins of the Liberal reforms, but research since 1950 has shown how important they were. Some organisations, such as the National Committee of Organised Labour on Old Age Pensions and the Women's Industrial Council (which publicised the evils of 'sweating') campaigned for social legislation. Most pressure groups, however, were concerned to defend particular, often commercial, sectional interests and thus tried to prevent certain types of social legislation, or to modify government proposals. The Friendly Societies – the institutional representatives of the self-help ethic among the working class – opposed state intervention on principle, and because they feared state competition for working-class savings. Demographic changes in the late nineteenth century undermined their position and forced them into conflict with successive governments over pensions [Gilbert, 1966; Treble, 1970]. Later, they were to clash with other powerful interests – the commercial insurance firms and the British Medical Association – over National Health Insurance. The Charity Organisation Society fought a rearguard action in support of a moral and individualist approach to poverty [Mowat, 1961]. Even within its ranks, however, there were signs that attitudes to state welfare measures were changing [Harris, 1972, 250, 301]. Some historians have emphasised a modern element in C.O.S. activity, its individual 'casework' approach to poverty, but others feel that separation of ideology and practice in this case is not satisfactory [Stedman Jones, 1971, 256–7; Fraser, 1973, 121–3].

38

Much more is now known about the role of the civil servants who helped to formulate and administer the Liberal welfare reforms. Of course, it was always appreciated that such men had considerable influence. Halévy referred to Sir George Askwith, Sir Hubert Llewellyn Smith and Sir Ernest Aves as 'secret dictators', who 'played a part probably more important than the great political figures who occupied the stage while they worked in the wings'. Some of them were far from secret at the time, and many have subsequently published autobiographical material, though it is only recently that systematic interest in their work has been renewed. It has become clear that the form of the Liberal welfare legislation was powerfully influenced by such men, and hence by their preconceptions and values. Their influence was, as might be expected, particularly great at those times when current remedies for social problems had obviously failed, and politicians were casting about for a new approach as, for example, in the case of unemployment policy between 1906 and 1909.

Of the civil servants who played a positive role in the origins of the Liberal reforms, many were Oxford graduates who then passed through the settlement house movement or helped Charles Booth with his poverty studies [T. S. and M. B. Simey, 1960, *101*]. Contact with the poor did not make such men 'soft' towards the claims on behalf of the poor which were being advanced in the early twentieth century. Beveridge and Llewellyn Smith took a very cool view of the unemployed. A common element in their approach, however, was the desire to quantify social problems. As social issues were transferred from a polemical to a statistical basis, their solution became acceptable to the official mind. These civil servants were not unaware of the value of social reforms as a means of social control, in part by integrating working-class organisations into the establishment [Winch, 1972, *39–40*].

Other civil servants are usually said to have hindered the process of reform. Those in the Local Government Board are credited with killing what little radicalism was left in John Burns, while those in the Home Office may have helped to immerse Herbert Gladstone in administrative routine. A more recent charge against these men is that they failed to come to terms with the new demands for statistical information on social issues. As a result the administration of social reform had to be undertaken by the Board of Trade which had the statistical expertise [Davidson, 1972]. This interpretation may do less than justice to the dynamic influence of the two heads of the latter department in the early years of the Liberal administration.

Finally, there were the inheritors of the Gladstonian tradition in the Treasury. They have been blamed for hindering state activity in the medical aspects of public health and restricting the development of the Local Government Board [MacLeod, 1967, 1968]. But Wright and Roseveare [1969] conclude that the Treasury did not exert inflexible control. Wright's criticism is rather that decisions were made on an *ad hoc* basis, with little or no systematic consideration.[14] Many Treasury officials were Liberals, but they opposed early Liberal social reforms fearing that their cost would force a subsequent government to introduce tariff reform. The insurance principle, however, enabled the Liberals to broaden the basis of taxation without departing from 'free trade'.

In the nineteenth century much of the expansion of public social welfare services was administered, not by central government, but by the local authorities. As a result, after 1880, local authority spending rose very rapidly, and by 1905 more than half of all government expenditure was being undertaken by them [Peacock and Wiseman, 1967, *208*]. But this expansion caused serious financial problems in certain areas. Suburban areas, with limited social needs and wealthy residents, tended to be lightly rated, while central urban areas, with considerable social deprivation and poor residents, were unable to cope. There were attempts to pool resources in some areas and central government grants, to some extent, took account of the needs of different localities, but serious inequalities remained. As far as social welfare services are concerned, therefore, by 1908 there was an impasse. If the Liberals wished to embark on social reform, they had really only two choices. They could reconstruct the whole basis of local authority finance, to iron out the major inequalities between areas, and provide sources of revenue which would grow to keep in step with rising expenditure, or they could provide new services nationally. But the reconstruction of local finance would give rise to major problems, as many local authorities stood to lose heavily by any redistribution. Chancellors of the Exchequer were also very reluctant to give local authorities expanding sources of revenue for fear that financial discipline might be weakened.

The alternative open to the government was to take over services which had previously been undertaken locally, or those which might have been given to the local authorities, had the nineteenth-century pattern been followed. So, in a sense, the expansion of central social services after 1908 was the inevitable result of the failure to reform local finance. There were, of course, other reasons why the Liberals provided old age pensions and health and unemployment insurance nationally. It was increasingly realised that problems like unemployment and personal health could only be tackled on a national scale. This was brought about, in part, by the failure of local attempts at solution, and by a clearer appreciation of the scale of the problems. There was also a strong desire on the part of most radicals, if not of the Liberal Party as a whole, to ensure that new services were provided separately from the Poor Law, which also had been under attack since the late nineteenth century.

The final institutional obstacle to the type of welfare reform proposed by the Liberals was the existence of the Poor Law. Virtually all of the new services, as Fraser has noted, were provided in some form or another under the existing Poor Law. Yet the Liberals, in the end, developed each of their reforms outside the Poor Law. Some of the reasons for this are fairly obvious. The Poor Law did carry a stigma, and was obviously socially discriminatory. But the Poor Law was continually being modified in the light of changing conditions. The Medical Relief (Disqualification Removal) Act of 1885 allowed those who sought only medical help to retain political rights, and Poor Law infirmaries were being widely used by the early twentieth century.

But Poor Law reform within the existing structure, or according to the schemes of the Royal Commission on the Poor Law, implied the reform of local government finance, and this was something which the Liberals did not face up to till 1914. Perhaps more important was the work of the economists and social investigators, which suggested, not that the Poor Law was 'inhumane or inefficient, but that it was irrelevant to the needs of an urban industrial society' [Rose, 1971, 237]. Marshall argued that cash payments to the poor need not necessarily depress wages.[15] Booth and Rowntree had shown that personal character was not the prime determinant of poverty.

The Poor Law itself was under attack from within. Some Boards of Guardians, encouraged by the Local Government Board and outside critics, were feeling their way towards a more humane treatment of the poor. Special consideration for 'respectable old people and cottage homes for children were results of this process. But within the Local Government Board there was a strong body of opinion which condemned the lack of uniformity of treatment and sought a return to the 'Principles of 1834'. Officials holding these views intended, according to Beatrice Webb, to use the Royal Commission on the Poor Laws to achieve this [Rose, 1971]. The Reports of the Royal Commission, however, may have helped to ensure the success of the Liberal plans for social reform outside the Poor Law, since they both envisaged changes in the administration of poor relief, abolishing the Boards of Guardians or relegating them to a subordinate role. The Guardians were, however, a substantial vested interest, and it may well have appeared much simpler to by-pass the problem of their future altogether.

4 The Process of Reform

(i) CHILDREN AND THE OLD

THE first group of measures of the Liberal period concerned children, and their history shows clearly the hesitant way in which the Liberal government embarked on social reform. School meals and medical inspection of school-children were both products of the climate of opinion created by the Boer War. The first of these was the more controversial since it raised the question whether those who received public assistance should be penalised as a result; whether the right of citizenship was dependent on the performance of certain social duties. As the conservative lawyer, Dicey, remarked, 'Why a man who first neglects his duty as a father and then defrauds the state should retain his full political rights is a question easier to ask than to answer.' Only when the prime cause of poverty was seen to be economic, and when poverty seemed to threaten the economic health of the nation, could an answer be given.

School meals had been provided to a limited extent by voluntary bodies during the nineteenth century, but it was not until the Boer War had highlighted the poor health of army recruits that the Royal Commission on Physical Training (Scotland) and the Interdepartmental Committee on Physical Deterioration recommended local authority assistance. (Both bodies also recommended the medical inspection of school-children.) The intervention of the Poor Law Guardians probably led to a decrease in the number of children being fed. After the election of 1906 the Labour Party, not the Liberals, took the lead in demanding that local authorities be compelled to feed needy children. The Liberals decided they could not oppose a private member's Bill and agreed to provide government time for the measure. The resulting Education (Provision of Meals) Act of 1906 did not compel local authorities to provide school meals, but it did allow expenditure out of the rates and ensured that the parents of children so assisted did not lose their political rights. Individualist objections were thus overborne by the desire to protect the children of the nation, because of considerations of national efficiency and pressure from the Labour Party.

Medical inspection of school-children owed something to backbench political pressure, but Sir Robert Morant, Permanent Secretary of the Board of Education, was responsible for its introduction, hidden among the clauses of the Education (Administrative Provisions) Act of 1907. Morant was concerned with national efficiency and wanted to use medical inspection as a means of revealing the mass of preventible disease, which would result in the acceptance of medical treatment. Like Sir George Newman, the Chief Medical Officer of the Board of Education, Morant was aware that educational, humanitarian and efficiency arguments supported the case for school meals and medical inspection and treatment.

They, and other social reformers within the Liberal Party, were able to take advantage of the changing attitudes to children around the turn of the century. Children had always had a special claim to protection from the rigours of industrial society, but as the birth rate fell their value as assets of the nation increased. The fall in the birth rate was greatest among the middle and upper classes and this led some contemporary personages to call for the restoration of the balance in society by the 'sterilisation of the unfit'. Few Liberals were prepared to go that far, but many agreed with Marshall that the current 'residuum' were almost beyond hope and that priority should be given to ensuring the health and efficiency of the next generation. The Children Act of 1908, which abolished committal of children to prison and added penalties for parents guilty of neglect, was a product of these changing attitudes and it passed easily through Parliament.[16] Similarly in the Education (Choice of Employment) Act of 1910 Morant attempted to cut down the intake of young people into dead-end jobs, through the provision of vocational guidance in schools.

44

Ways of assisting the old had also been under consideration for most of the last quarter of the nineteenth century. Two types of proposal were discussed. One derived largely from Charles Booth's poverty studies and a series of government enquiries which showed that poverty was particularly severe among the old. Booth believed that the majority of the working class would find it impossible to save enough to provide for their old age. Accordingly non-contributory pensions, financed out of general taxation, should be given to all those over seventy. Booth's plan attracted working-class support, but its main drawback was its cost, estimated at a minimum of £16 million in 1900. The other proposal is usually associated with the Rev. W. L. Blackley, who argued for a national insurance scheme to provide sickness benefits and pensions, not on the basis of statistical evidence about poverty, but in the belief that such provision would reduce the poor rates. Some historians emphasise the modern element in this suggestion – the idea that individual contribution carried an automatic right to benefit [Collins, 1965, 23]. Blackley, however, probably saw it as a means of state encouragement to working-class thrift. He had, however, virtually ignored the administrative problems of collecting contributions and the objections of the Friendly Societies to any state intervention in their field.

The first politician of note to take up old age pensions, for reasons which are still not entirely clear, was Joseph Chamberlain.* He proposed a contributory scheme which reserved an important role for the Friendly Societies. Nevertheless they remained opposed both to the contributory principle and to the state subsidy, fearing that the first might render them superfluous and the second might lead to the nationalisation of their funds. But the Friendly Societies were under financial pressure, as members continued to live longer and draw sickness benefits which became disguised pensions. From the 1890s their attitude to state pensions slowly began to change [Gilbert, 1966, *179*; Treble, 1970, *280–8*].

* Chamberlain's own brand of social concern can be traced back to his days as a Birmingham city councillor, but by the 1890s it had strong Bismarckian overtones : See E. P. Hennock, *Fit and Proper Persons* (1973) pp. 173–4; Semmel (1960) p. 92.

Chamberlain may have lost interest in pensions as a result of this opposition, but popular pressure began to build up in the late 1890s, partly because New Zealand had introduced pensions in 1898. The National Committee of Organised Labour on Old Age Pensions was set up and, though it was dependent on middle-class finance, it attracted trade union support. In 1899 a Treasury Committee was examining the cost of a non-contributory pensions scheme, similar in many respects to that finally introduced by the Liberals in 1908. It is arguable that had not the Boer War intervened pensions might well have been introduced a decade earlier. In fact the War and its aftermath prevented serious discussion of pensions for the next six years, though in that time popular pressure still continued, and some Friendly Societies came reluctantly to the conclusion that a non-contributory pension scheme might be in their interests.

As late as 1906 the Liberals, as a party, were not committed to old age pensions, though individual candidates at the election were [Russell, 1973, 65]. There is still some doubt though as to when, and why, the commitment to pensions was made. Gilbert, in a rather strained interpretation of the evidence, suggests that consideration of pensions began early in 1906 to provide balance to the Liberal programme and to meet the charge, from the Tories, that the Liberals were the prisoners of the socialists [Gilbert, 1966, 203]. F. H. Stead believed that pressure from a deputation of Liberal and Labour Members of Parliament in November 1906 forced the hands of Asquith and Campbell-Bannerman. Fraser, like Gilbert, stresses the importance of the Colne Valley and Jarrow by-elections in 1907, when Liberal candidates were defeated by Labour men. He takes this as a criticism of the lack of Liberal social policy [Fraser, 1973, 142]. However, as early as July 1906, Asquith's private secretary was collecting data on pensions, and a proposal was put before the Cabinet in December 1906. The Cabinet accepted the creation of a fund for the provision of non-contributory pensions in April 1907, which suggests that the by-elections played no serious part in the Liberal calculations.[17]

The motives for the introduction of old age pensions were very mixed. Ideas of national efficiency or, except very indirectly, wider economic considerations played little part.* Pensions could be interpreted as an anti-socialist measure in the Bismarckian sense, though when the German example was brought up during the Parliamentary debate, it was usually only in support of the case for contributory pensions. Popular pressure, though important in 1899 and subsequently, proved easily resistible, especially between 1903 and 1906. It is unlikely that Asquith's initial decision to prepare material on old age pensions owed much to outside pressures, though the Cabinet decision to go ahead may have done. Old age pensions were, to some extent, a product of statistical investigation which proved the extent of poverty among the old and the impossibility of attributing it solely to moral failing. Humanitarian considerations were probably stronger in the case of pensions than in any other Liberal measures, though Asquith and many of his colleagues saw pensions more in terms of the duty of the state towards its citizens, as redefined by T. H. Green and his successors. The pension scheme marked the end of the first phase of Liberal policy. The second phase, which was perhaps less of a break than some historians have suggested, began with a renewed attack on unemployment.

(ii) UNEMPLOYMENT AND MINIMUM WAGES

Though Churchill referred to unemployment as 'the untrodden field of politics' in 1908, it had in fact been the subject of debate and various forms of government action since the 1880s. In that decade unemployment was recognised as a chronic problem of the British economy, and some writers began to see it, rather than bad housing, as the root cause of crime, vagrancy, prostitution and poverty [K. D. Brown, 1971a; Harris, 1972, 4]. Prior to this unemployment tended to be regarded as a temporary phenomenon, or one confined to specific industries, as was the case during the Lancashire cotton famine.

* Marshall had argued before the Royal Commission on the Aged Poor in 1893 that payments to the poor need not depress wages, since they would tend to raise efficiency and levels of consumption. Asquith does not appear to have made use of this argument.

The economic crisis of the mid-1880s inspired the new concern about unemployment. The focus of attention was London, where the external pressures on the British economy were reinforced by the structural decline of traditional industries under competition from expanded factory production in the provinces [Stedman Jones, 1971, *281*]. The coincidence of structural, cyclical and seasonal crises led to riots by unemployed workers during the winters of 1886 and 1887. The riots are sometimes seen as the cause of the famous Chamberlain circular of March 1886, which encouraged local authorities to provide relief work for the unemployed, entirely separate from the Poor Law [Gilbert, 1966, *38*; K. D. Brown, 1971*a*]. Harris, on the other hand, argues that the riots were treated at the time as a problem of public order, rather than social distress, though she notes that Chamberlain's motive in issuing the circular was to reduce public sympathy for the unemployed and to enable greater strictness to be applied to the loafer or confirmed pauper [Harris, 1972, *56*, *76*].

Whatever interpretation is placed on the Chamberlain circular, there is no doubt that unemployment became and remained a subject of public concern. During each subsequent trade depression – 1892–5, 1903–5 and 1908–9 – governments were forced by renewed political agitation to reconsider existing legislation and administrative arrangements. Attempts to find remedies appeared to be handicapped by lack of information about unemployment. In the case of old age pensions good statistical evidence was available, but unemployment was a more complex issue. Some historians argue that improvements in statistical knowledge were a precondition for legislation [Davidson, 1972], though Harris has shown how such improvements were themselves largely a product of legislative and administrative reform [Harris, 1972, *47*].

Before 1900 two types of proposal to deal with unemployment were widely discussed. Socialists led the demand for a legal eight-hour day as a means of work-sharing, but when this was tried in government departments and private firms little increase in employment was forthcoming, since productivity often rose. The other proposal, canvassed by Charles Booth, was for the removal of the lower strata of the poor to labour colonies, to reduce the competition for employment with other groups, who would thus experience a rise in earnings. Those in the colonies were to be employed at public expense, or retrained. Others had different intentions for labour colonies. Some Poor Law officials wanted penal establishments for habitual paupers. George Lansbury, on the other hand, saw labour colonies as a potential experiment in community reconstruction under popular control. The revival of trade in the latter half of the 1890s turned attention away from these schemes before some of their obvious deficiencies had been fully explored.

After the Boer War, socialist organisations once again took the lead in organising agitation about unemployment [K. D. Brown, 1971a]. Local authorities began relief work schemes and, in the winter of 1904–5, the President of the Local Government Board, Walter Long, proposed to co-ordinate and extend their activities. His intention was to provide for the respectable able-bodied, and also to head off the demand for a national measure to deal with unemployment [Harris, 1972, 153]. Long admitted later that he had been driven to introduce the Unemployed Workmen Act of 1905 because of popular pressure on the local authorities, which they in turn transmitted to central government [K. D. Brown, 1971a].

The Act in practice was a failure. The idea of providing relief work for temporarily unemployed artisans was discredited. Beveridge found that the bulk of those relieved were those who were normally on the verge of distress. Chronic underemployment was as much a problem as unemployment. The Act also demonstrated the failure of charitable casework to deal with the extent of unemployment, and of local authority action. As Percy Alden and Keir Hardie had argued since the 1890s, local authority resources were inversely related to the extent of unemployment in their areas. Therefore a national measure, and one which operated in the context of the normal labour market, was the only solution yet untried, short of acceptance of socialist remedies on the one hand, or tariff reform on the other.

In 1906 the Liberals came to power with no party commitment to tackle unemployment beyond enquiry and experiment, but they could not sustain this position for long. Growing socialist

49

agitation in support of the 'right to work', together with trade union pressure for action to relieve unemployment were, for the first time, reflected in Parliament by a substantial group of Labour members. Pressure increased as unemployment rose to its highest level since 1886. With the depression came the possibility of the revival of the appeal of tariff reform as a means of reducing unemployment. The Liberals lost seven seats to the Conservatives during the first nine months of 1908, and, in the short run, this was more of an immediate political threat than the spectacular losses to Labour at Colne Valley and Jarrow.

Caught between the hammer and the anvil Liberals could not continue to take refuge behind the Royal Commission on the Poor Laws, whose forthcoming report was expected to deal with the subject of unemployment. The Fabian-inspired minority was known, thanks to judicious leaks by Beatrice Webb, to favour fundamental interference with the labour market. Even the less radical majority was prepared to recommend labour exchanges, unemployment insurance, training for the unemployed, and better technical education. These views were made known to leading politicians, including Asquith, Haldane, Churchill and Balfour. The reconstruction of the Liberal administration, on the death of Campbell-Bannerman, brought Lloyd George and Churchill to the fore, and the latter came briefly under the influence of the Webbs in 1908. It was partly on their advice that he took William Beveridge, who had already made himself an authority on labour exchanges and unemployment, into the Board of Trade.

The problem facing the Liberals from 1908 to 1909 was to frame a programme which would make the minimum alterations in the normal workings of the labour market to satisfy individualists, economists and industrialists. It also had to be largely self-financing in order to avoid unacceptable increases in direct taxation or the reintroduction of tariffs. Some Liberals were concerned that an expensive social reform programme would alienate their lower-middle-class support. It also had to be separate from the Poor Law, yet cater for the vast mass of workers not organised in trade unions, without involving civil servants in discriminating between the poor individually. This is why the insurance principle was so important, because it provided both the finance and an automatic means of discrimination, not, as some writers have suggested, because moral issues were irrelevant to the social reform of the New Liberalism [for differing views on this point, see J. Brown, 1971, *112–13*; Harris, 1972, *313–14*; Fraser, 1973, *150, 160*]. Finally, the programme had to be acceptable enough, in conjunction with other measures, including tax changes, to a sufficient proportion of the working class in order to divert their attention from Fabian or more extreme socialist solutions [Petter, 1973, *48*].

In the 1909 Budget Lloyd George set out the results of Liberal deliberations. There were three main proposals. The normal working of the labour market was to be improved by means of voluntary labour exchanges.* The distress caused by unemployment was to be relieved by a limited scheme of unemployment insurance. Most radical in intention, if not in results, was the plan to reduce the severity of trade fluctuations, and to make better use of national resources in the long run, by afforestation and development schemes.

Labour exchanges were developed by Beveridge and Churchill out of the former's experience with the Unemployed Workmen Act. The origins of, and responsibility for, the serious consideration of unemployment insurance by the Liberals are still somewhat obscure. Lloyd George claimed the original idea following his famous visit to Germany in August 1908 – but Germany did not have unemployment insurance. Some historians argue that Churchill's drive and initiative was the important factor, and that, in his mind, unemployment insurance and labour exchanges were only part of a concerted attack on the problem of unemployment, sickness, and old age [Churchill, 1969, *895–8*; Fraser, 1973, *162*]. There is evidence that he was considering such ideas in 1907.[18] Others now point to the statistical work being undertaken by the Board of Trade as the necessary germ from which the Liberal legislation was to grow.

* The Webbs wanted compulsory labour exchanges, except for those in regular jobs who found themselves temporarily unemployed. Casual and seasonal jobs were to be dovetailed through the National Exchange.

By late 1908 serious preparatory work was under way in the Board of Trade, but it was decided to combine unemployment and health insurance in one Bill. The health insurance scheme was complementary to the unemployment one, which could not have worked had those who were out of work through illness or invalidity been included.

From the outset the scheme was conceived as a limited one, to provide insurance cover against cyclical unemployment in a narrow range of industries which responded to depression by laying off workers rather than resorting to short-time working. Benefits were to be kept low to avoid encouraging unemployment. The idea of deterrence lingered on. Above all only economic risks could be insured against, and claims resulting from personal misbehaviour were to be rigorously excluded. Churchill argued against the last provision, feeling that the payment of contributions established the right to benefit, but he was overruled. The moral attitude of the nineteenth century was not absent from the social legislation of the twentieth. Such provisions in the Act seemed to support Belloc's assertion that collectivism was leading to the servile state, where the worker, in return for social benefits, would have his working life governed by positive law [Belloc, 1912].

The final part of the Liberal programme was the Development Fund set up in 1909. The intention was to use it to stimulate expenditure by other parties, especially the local authorities. They were to be encouraged and assisted to carry out public works which should be scheduled as far as possible for the depression phases of the trade cycle. It was hoped that this would help to reduce the severity of cyclical fluctuations.

Other Liberal legislation on industrial matters included the Trades Disputes Act, restoring the legal immunity of trade unions, and the Workmen's Compensation Act of 1906. Both were a product of the electoral links between the Liberal and Labour parties and contained little novelty. Minimum-wage legislation was a more radical step, and the two measures in this field had very different backgrounds. The Trade Boards Act of 1909, under which minumum wages and maximum hours could be fixed in a group of 'sweated trades', was the result of pressure from women's organisations; individual politicians, including Ramsay MacDonald and Sir Charles Dilke, quoting American and Australian practice, respectively; and a public campaign mounted by the *Daily Mail*. The trade unions played little part [Roberts, 1958, *217*]. The Trade Boards Act protected the weak and ill-organised, but minimum-wage legislation for coal miners followed a campaign by a highly organised group of workers. In 1908 the miners gained a national eight-hour day, which they might have obtained much earlier but for divisions between the miners in different coalfields. Faced with a national coal strike in 1912, on the issue of a minimum wage, the government reluctantly gave way, though they refused to insert specific figures for wages and sought to ensure that no general conclusions would be drawn from the miners' case

Both minimum-wage Acts seemed to raise the principle of a general minimum wage. Fraser claims that the Trade Boards Act was the result of Churchill's conversion to the idea of a 'national minimum' as proposed by the Webbs, while Emy argues that Lloyd George, in his land campaign in 1913, endorsed the idea of a national minimum wage [Emy, 1973, *271*; Fraser, 1973, *158*]. As a result of the legislation of 1909 and 1912 the Liberals were certainly being driven in that direction, but a substantial body of opinion within the Party remained opposed to such a measure.

In all industrial matters, especially unemployment, the Liberals were more subject to effective popular pressure than on most other social issues. The fact that there were competing proposals – the right to work, nationalisation, and a national minimum, on the one hand, tariff reform on the other – forced them to produce the series of measures which made limited alterations in the working of the labour market and retained free trade. In principle, many of the Liberal measures were capable of extension, but it remains a matter of speculation whether the particular series of compromises evolved could have formed a successful industrial programme. Nevertheless, as Harris has pointed out, some of the practical experience of the New Liberalism was forgotten in the interwar years, and lessons had to be learned again at much greater social cost [Harris, 1972, *368*].

(iii) HEALTH INSURANCE

Unlike unemployment insurance, which was very largely a response to working-class pressure, health insurance – the other part of the National Insurance Act of 1911 – derived much more directly from the concern for national efficiency at the turn of the twentieth century. Up to that time, state intervention in matters of health had developed along two fairly distinct lines. Firstly, there were public health measures designed to cope with major emergencies such as cholera, and to improve environmental conditions which contributed to ill-health and poverty. In the 1880s with the renewed interest in poverty, it might have been expected that further development of public health legislation by central government would have followed, but the national debate had relatively little effect on the Local Government Board and its Medical Department, and Treasury resistance seems to have weakened what little desire existed to expand preventative measures [MacLeod, 1967]. The other form of state intervention was the treatment of ill-health in its various forms. The expansion of medical services within the Poor Law had been continuous since the mid-nineteenth century. Medical treatment did not lend itself to the strict application of the principle of less eligibility, and, inevitably, treatment of the sick in Poor Law institutions was often better than the very poor could obtain elsewhere.

In the 1890s public concern about matters of health declined, but the Boer War and the subsequent investigations revived it. Some believed that the progressive degeneration of the health of the working classes had set in. The Interdepartmental Committee on Physical Deterioration of 1904 scotched this extreme view, but a running debate, between social Darwinists and social investigators, and members of the medical profession, kept the question before the public for much of the first decade of the century. Concern was initially focused on the possibility of doing something to rescue the next generation, and led directly to medical inspection and school meals. However, the Report confirmed Rowntree's conclusions, in his study of York, that 'a low standard of health prevails among the working classes. It therefore becomes obvious that the widespread existence of poverty in an industrial country like our own must seriously retard its development.'[19] Various groups began to argue that something ought to be done about the current generation.

Progressive employers were increasingly concerned about the health and efficiency of their employees. They also feared Labour Party proposals to extend Workmen's Compensation to all sickness and accidents, with the cost being borne entirely by employers. Moreover the Labour Party was groping towards the idea of a comprehensive health service provided at the best medical standards then available, though according to Marwick its proposals had no direct influence on legislation [Marwick, 1967, 386–7]. Even the medical profession, which had often resisted state intervention, found itself in an ambiguous position.

Many doctors provided medical treatment under contract to the Friendly Societies. While this form of practice could be lucrative, competition among doctors had forced the rates down. Meanwhile Friendly Society practice was in competition with private doctors for those patients who could afford to pay fees, while, at the other end of the scale, it was failing to reach the mass of the workers. In 1905 a British Medical Association Report on Contract Practice actually recommended a public medical service to meet the needs of those just above the Poor Law. The intention was to try to obtain a state service which would give the doctors independence of the Friendly Societies, and a secure and substantial income. The hospitals were in even worse straits. In 1910 the *British Medical Journal* commented that 'The perilous condition of general hospital funds will . . ., sooner rather than later, compel boards of management to accept state control in return for state assistance, on any terms the state chooses to impose.' The doctors had not been converted to enthusiastic support for state action, but their economic position made them much more receptive to interference than they would normally have been [Brand, 1965, 216–17].

Both reports of the Royal Commission on the Poor Laws recommended state action in the field of public and private health. The Minority Report called for an attack on the sickness which caused poverty. The 'prevention of sickness' rather than the 'relief of distress due to ill health' was their aim. Accordingly a Public Health Authority should be set up to co-ordinate measures to prevent ill-health and care for those who did fall ill. The Majority also wanted improved health measures, including a network of provident dispensaries. These were to be financed by voluntary contributions, and they tentatively suggested invalidity insurance as a valuable addition. They, too, wanted administrative co-ordination of the various agencies in the field, though they were not prepared to consider the thoroughgoing interference in the lives of individuals proposed by the Minority.

By the end of the first decade of the twentieth century, therefore, there was a strong consensus on the need for action to improve the health of the individual, but little agreement as to the best method to proceed. Should poverty due to sickness be relieved, or should there be a thoroughgoing extension of public health measures and attack on the causes of sickness? Either approach was consistent with arguments for improving national efficiency, though the latter approach implied a longer-term solution and higher expenditure. The Liberals decided, partly for ideological reasons, and partly because they calculated that they would have to work through existing agencies in the field, that they would proceed by relieving poverty due to sickness.

Originally in 1908 Lloyd George intended to extend the pensions scheme to cover widows, orphans, and the chronic sick, whose plight, he believed, was often worse than that of the old. Historians agree that his visit to Germany in the autumn was the inspiration for a more complete health insurance scheme, which would also provide for those temporarily unemployed as a result of illness. In the 1909 Budget and the proposals for a coalition between Liberals and Conservatives in 1910, this contribution of insurance to national efficiency was brought out. This aspect grew in importance as the complex series of negotiations on the insurance Bill continued. The industrial insurance lobby, with its interest in death benefits, forced Lloyd George to drop his idea for widows' and orphans' pensions. Control of medical treatment was taken from the Friendly Societies and given to appointed Insurance Committees to propitiate the medical profession, and the financial difficulties of the ordinary general practitioners were used as a lever to bring them into a scheme, which the leadership of the British Medical Association disliked [Gilbert, 1966, chaps 6, 7].

In its final form, Part I of the National Insurance Act did not seriously attempt to tackle the causes of ill-health. Provision was made for sanatoria and for expenditure on medical research, and in 1914 Lloyd George made grants to local authorities for nursing and clinical services. Some of his liberal colleagues, especially Haldane in the House of Lords, did stress the preventative elements in the Act [Searle, 1971, 255]. Health insurance was, thus, an uneasy compromise or, as Lloyd George called it, 'an ambulance wagon'. He looked forward to the time when the state would accept full responsibility for provision for sickness, breakdown and unemployment, separate from the Poor Law, but his 'temporary expedient', in fact, set the pattern for the social legislation of the next generation [Fraser, 1973, 156–7].

(iv) FISCAL POLICY

Liberal fiscal policy ought to be considered as part of the process of social reform. In 1906 the Liberals were committed to a reduction of government expenditure in the classic nineteenth-century tradition, and to proposals for the redistribution of the burden of taxation by progressive taxation and taxes on land. Asquith planned to introduce both of these measures, but Treasury opposition meant that their introduction was postponed till 1909, by which time the dream of reducing expenditure had vanished.

The idea of progressive direct taxation was not new in 1906. Sir William Harcourt had originally planned to graduate income tax in 1894, taking his stand on social justice rather than on the views of the academic economists. By the turn of the century, however, orthodox economists had provided some guarded justification for the redistribution of income by public expenditure and taxation. Edgeworth used the idea of the declining marginal utility of income to justify progressive taxation, though not all his colleagues were converted. Sidgwick, Bastable and Marshall opposed progressive taxation to varying degrees, though

Marshall gradually changed his mind [Shehab, 1953, *199*; Winch, 1972, *41–2*). Under-consumptionists, like J. A. Hobson, were more forthright, arguing that the existence of monopoly in various forms meant that the redistribution of income in society had departed from the optimum. Therefore redistribution by the state could contribute to economic efficiency by increasing consumption. Notice that Hobson's first justification for income redistribution was efficiency, not social justice, and he was prepared to support trade union action, progressive taxation and attacks on monopoly to achieve this end [Emy, 1973, *106–11*]. Socialist support for redistributive taxation was much more based on the case for social justice. Some writers have argued that from this time major differences in principle developed between the parties on taxation, income redistribution and social expenditure. Emy, for example, argues that by 1914 the Liberals had accepted that 'productive expenditure, emanating from the state, was a necessary condition for the further development of society'. To finance this, progressive taxation was necessary, and justifiable on grounds of efficiency and social justice. The Conservatives, however, remained attached to the nineteenth-century notion of equality of sacrifice and payment by classes in proportion to the benefits they received [Emy, 1972]. There is something to be said for this distinction, though it cannot be pushed too far. Some Conservatives supported social expenditure, especially on education, and progressive taxation, while many Liberals, who accepted both in theory, were appalled at the practice under Lloyd George.

There was a difference, however, between the parties in the methods of financing social reform. Many Conservatives wanted tariff reform, *inter alia*, as a means of paying for social measures. Tariff reform would broaden the basis of taxation and ensure that relatively low taxes, on foodstuffs and other items, would yield sufficient revenue. Liberals argued, as they had done in the nineteenth century, that tariffs would raise the cost of living, hinder trade, and divert resources from their most productive uses. They preferred direct taxation which, they argued, had less effect on trade and enterprise. Moreover progressive direct taxation would enable sufficient revenue to be raised, and, if the weight of increased taxation was concentrated on unearned incomes, from land and other sources, this would have the minimum effect on the growth of capital.

In practice the differences between the parties, both on the principle of income redistribution and on methods of finance, may have been somewhat less than the fury of contemporary debate, and some historical comments, have suggested. Though old age pensions were financed out of general taxation, when it came to the second major piece of social legislation, on health and unemployment, the Liberals decided on a contributory system. Economists disagree on the incidence of insurance contributions. American writers, on the whole, tend to regard both employer and employee contributions as being deductions from wages, while some British economists have argued that the employers' contributions are passed on to the consumer in higher prices. This disagreement reflects a contemporary debate over the incidence of contributions in 1911. The Treasury tended to take the former line, while Beveridge argued that the consumer paid the employer's contribution. Churchill, however, told one group of employers that they would be able to pass the cost of their contributions on to their workers by reducing the rate of growth of wages. Though there is this disagreement, economists are agreed that the insurance system redistributes income within social classes rather than between them. To this extent, tariff reform and social insurance have similar effects. Some historians have tended to take Lloyd George's slogan of '9d for 4d' at its face value, but those members of Labour and socialist organisations, who drew attention to the regressive effects of the insurance contributions, would find support among modern economists.

5 Conclusion

EACH of the Liberal reforms had its own specific origins and prehistory. Some historians prefer to see them as individual solutions to particular social problems, not as part of a wider movement. At one level of analysis this is perfectly reasonable. The failure of previous social measures, or the lack of them, combined with exposure and analysis of each social problem, led to the proposal and adoption of new solutions. But 'failure' implies standards against which it is measured, and a political will to achieve success. As Tawney put it, 'the continuance of social evils is not due to the fact that we do not know what is right, but to the fact that we prefer to continue doing what is wrong' [quoted in Rose, 1972, 52].

There were many participants in the creation of the Liberal reforms who had no thought of creating a 'welfare state' of the type which developed in Britain after 1945. Indeed many of the Liberals of 1906–14 would have been appalled by that prospect. Moreover the measures adopted always had a tactical significance in the parliamentary struggle between the parties : each was a response to a specific electoral situation, as was the case with the decision to proceed with labour exchanges and unemployment insurance in 1908–9. But this does not mean that social reform can be completely explained in such terms. Key figures, like Lloyd George and Churchill, looked beyond individual pieces of legislation towards the creation of a society in which the worst ravages of poverty would be eliminated. They saw the strategic importance of welfare measures which would, at one and the same time, act as an antidote to socialism and hinder the polarisation of the electorate between Labour and Conservatives in Britain, contribute to the efficiency of the British economy by preventing the physical and mental deterioration of the workers, and provide a measure of social justice which would

61

help to attract working-class votes without alienating the middle classes [Petter, 1973, *46*].

The welfare reforms did not, however, originate exclusively in the heroic vision of a few Liberal individuals. There were other competing proposals for social reform in Britain in the late nineteenth and early twentieth centuries. Liberal Unionists sought to achieve substantially similiar results to the Liberals, though by different fiscal and legislative means. The working classes, or rather organisations representing them, also had proposals for social reform which sometimes started from different assumptions and pointed to widely different conclusions. Part of the problem is to explain why the Liberal solutions were adopted; but the more fundamental question is, why were all these various proposals under simultaneous discussion? This is the ultimate justification for concentrating on the common influences on the origins of the reforms. As was noted at the outset, other societies, facing similar problems, adopted similar measures, and the British social reforms have to be seen in the wider context of the response of capitalist societies to the experience of economic growth.

Much of the research which has been surveyed here has improved our knowledge of various aspects of this response. Much more is now known about the influence of economic, political, ideological and institutional changes. The desire to retain as much as possible of the existing capitalist economic system, at a time when it was under increasing pressure from within and without, seems to have been the most important motive in the origins of the Liberal reforms. The 'class abatement' aspects, as Marshall called them, were clearest in measures dealing with unemployment. As time passed and other measures to incorporate the working-class leadership into the political establishment took effect, social reform could more readily take the form of concessions to legitimate popular demand. Changing attitudes to poverty, the redefinition of the relationship between the state and its citizens, and improved statistical knowledge also played a part in the process of reform, but humanitarian opinion, by itself, seems to have achieved less than an earlier generation of historians believed.

62

Some major gaps in knowledge remain. Popular attitudes to the welfare reforms among the rank and file of various organisations and those who remained unorganised are still unknown. Research is needed on a regional and occupational rather than a national basis. The influence of business interests in the process of reform is still largely unexplored, and cannot be assessed solely in terms of opposition to tax changes and to the National Insurance Bill. The extent to which the reforms carried out the intentions of their originators also needs to be carefully studied. Attitudes to the welfare reforms have often been conditioned by the acceptance of some of the more quotable phrases of politicians. The final form of legislation and the administrative process by which this legislation was implemented often differed quite considerably from these statements of intention. Finally, the international comparisons which will illuminate more clearly the unique features of the Liberal reforms in Britain are only just beginning.

In the end, however, when this knowledge is available, it will still be necessary to put the reforms back into the context of late Victorian and Edwardian society. It is not sufficient to continue accumulating fragments of knowledge about specific aspects of the reforms. They will have to be related to the other changes in the economy and society which governments increasingly sought to control. There is a need for a return to the breadth of vision of Halévy and some of his predecessors, who were aware that social reform was only one part of a search for ways of preserving British imperial society.

References

1. R. M. Titmuss, 'Poverty Versus Inequality', in *Poverty*, ed. J. L. and J. K. Roach (1972) p. 321; [George, 1973, chap. 1].
2. P. Cutwright, 'Political Structure, Economic Development and National Social Security Programs', *American Journal of Sociology*, 70 (1965).
3. J. Saville, 'The Welfare State: an Historical Approach', *The New Reasoner*, 1 (1957–8); D. Wedderburn, 'Facts and Theories of the Welfare State', in *The Socialist Register*, ed. R. Miliband and J. Saville (1965).
4. F. Rogers, *Labour, Life and Literature: Some Memories of Sixty Years* (1913); F. H. Stead, *How Old Age Pensions Began To Be* (n.d.).
5. Helen F. Hohman, *The Development of Social Insurance and Minimum Wage Legislation in Great Britain* (Boston, 1933); and [Brend, 1917].
6. R. W. Harris, *Not so Humdrum* (1939); [Tallents 1943].
7. D. Roberts, *The Victorian Origins of the British Welfare State* (New Haven, 1960).
8. R. MacLeod, 'Social Policy and the Floating Population', *Past and Present*, 35 (1966); [MacLeod, 1967].
9. J. Brown, 'The Appointment of the 1905 Poor Law Commission', *Bulletin of the Institute of Historical Research*, 42 (1969), and debate with K. D. Brown in ibid. 44 (1971).
10. N. Blewett, 'The Franchise in the United Kingdom, 1885–1918', *Past and Present*, 32 (1965) 28.
11. K. Coates and R. Silburn, *Poverty: the Forgotten Englishmen* (1970) pp. 136–56.
12. S. Reynolds, B. and T. Woolley, *Seems So* (1911) pp. 315–16.
13. D. C. M. Platt similarly interprets late Victorian imperial expansion. Platt, 'Economic Factors in British Policy During the New Imperialism', *Past and Present*, 39 (1968).
14. M. Wright, 'Treasury Control, 1854–1914' in *Studies in the Growth of Nineteenth-Century Government*, ed. G. Sutherland (1972).

15. A. Marshall, *Official Papers* (1926) p. 249.
16. H. Samuel, *Memoirs* (1945) pp. 54–6.
17. Public Record Office, Cab. 41, Cabinet Letter, 13 April 1907.
18. H. Wilson Harris, *J. A. Spender* (1946) p. 80.
19. B. S. Rowntree, *Poverty: A Study of Town Life* (1901; 4th ed. 1902) p. 303.

Bibliography

AN enormous literature already exists on the origins of the Liberal welfare reforms. Most of the items mentioned in this bibliography are modern historical works dealing with the reforms in a British context, but in addition some of the more important contemporary works, and a few general surveys of welfare programmes and policies, are included. The books by B. B. Gilbert, J. F. Harris and F. L. Pryor contain excellent bibliographies, while the footnotes in Halévy, Emy and Rimlinger refer to a considerable range of additional primary and secondary sources of different types. All works are published in London, unless indicated otherwise.

P. Adelman, *The Rise of the Labour Party, 1880–1945* (1972).
A good, brief survey, which takes account of recent research.

H. Belloc, *The Servile State* (1912).
A contemporary forecast of the likely outcome of collectivist social legislation.

W. H. Beveridge, *Unemployment: a Problem of Industry* (1909, 1930).
A pioneering study of the economic causes of unemployment, by the man who inspired the introduction of labour exchanges.

W. H. Beveridge, *Power and Influence* (1953).
His autobiography. Not entirely reliable in details, but a useful source for the origins of labour exchanges.

J. L. Brand, *Doctors and the State* (Baltimore, 1965).
Useful on the origins of health insurance.

W. A. Brend, *Health and the State* (1917).
An early, critical account of health insurance forms part of this valuable study.

A. Briggs, *Social Thought and Social Action: a Study of the Work of Seebohm Rowntree, 1871–1954* (1961).
Referred to in the text as (1961a).

A. Briggs, 'The Welfare State in Historical Perspective', *Archives Européennes de Sociologie*, 2 (1961). (1961*b*).
A now classic article, widely quoted in later work.

J. Brown, 'Charles Booth and Labour Colonies', *Economic History Review*, 21 (1968).
Argues that Booth's moral preoccupations influenced his work.

J. Brown, 'Social Judgements and Social Policy', *Economic History Review*, 24 (1971).
A reply to Lummis (1971).

K. D. Brown, 'Conflict in Early British Welfare Policy : the Case of the Unemployed Workmen Bill of 1905', *Journal of Modern History*, 43 (1971). (1971*a*).
Argues that working-class pressure was responsible for the origins and the introduction of the Bill.

K. D. Brown, *Labour and Unemployment 1900–14* (Newton Abbot, 1971). (1971*b*).
A study of the activities of political organisations and the trade unions. Needs to be read in conjunction with Harris (1972).

M. Bruce, *The Coming of the Welfare State* (3rd ed., 1966).
Widely used, but not always well-organised, account.

A. Bullock and M. Shock, *The Liberal Tradition: from Fox to Keynes* (1956, Oxford University Press, 1967 ed.).
A selection of documents, particularly useful on the changing attitudes of the late nineteenth century.

H. N. Bunbury (ed.), *Lloyd George's Ambulance Wagon: Being the Memoirs of W. J. Braithwaite, 1911–12* (1957).
A partisan account of the origins of health insurance by the civil servant who carried out most of the preparatory work. Needs to be used with care, see Gilbert (1966).

J. A. M. Caldwell, 'The Genesis of the Ministry of Labour', *Public Administration*, 37 (1959).
Contains material on labour exchanges and unemployment insurance.

R. S. Churchill, *W. S. Churchill, The Young Statesman, 1901–14* (1967).

R. S. Churchill, *Companion Volume*, in 3 parts (1969).
Together these are an invaluable source for Churchill's brief career as a social reformer.

W. S. Churchill, *Liberalism and the Social Problem* (1909).
One of several good manifestos of the 'New Liberalism'.

P. F. Clarke, *Lancashire and the New Liberalism* (Cambridge University Press, 1971).
Argues, on the basis of Lancashire evidence, that the Liberal Party had achieved a viable position in the new class politics of the early twentieth century.

P. F. Clarke, 'The Electoral Sociology of Modern Britain', *History,* 57 (1972).
Develops some of the ideas in Clarke (1971) against the background of some sociological interpretations of recent British electoral history.

D. Collins, 'The Introduction of Old Age Pensions in Great Britain', *Historical Journal,* 8 (1965).
Factual account. To be supplemented by Gilbert (1966) and Treble (1970).

A. J. Culyer, *The Economics of Social Policy* (1973).
Discusses the theories of income redistribution through social policy, of Hochman and Rodgers, Downs and Tulloch.

G. Dangerfield, *The Strange Death of Liberal England* (1936).
Controversial description of the crises of British society on the eve of the First World War. The new orthodoxy tends to disparage the notion of an interconnected series of crises, probably wrongly.

R. Davidson, 'Llewellyn Smith, the Labour Department and Government Growth', in *Studies in the Growth of 19th Century Government,* ed. G. Sutherland (1972).
Argues that the statistical expertise of the Board of Trade under Llewellyn Smith made it the natural department to administer social reform measures.

H. V. Emy, 'The Land Campaign; Lloyd George as a Social Reformer, 1909–14', in *Lloyd George: 12 Essays,* ed. A. J. P. Taylor (1971).

H. V. Emy, 'The Impact of Financial Policy on English Party Politics Before 1914', *Historical Journal,* 15 (1972).
Suggests that financial policy marked a clear division between the Liberal and Conservative parties.

H. V. Emy, *Liberals, Radicals and Social Politics 1892–1914* (Cambridge University Press, 1973).

A study in ideas and their effects on policy. Full of information, but not well organised, and judgements are occasionally suspect.

D. Fraser, *The Evolution of the British Welfare State* (1973).
The best brief modern account, particularly good and clear on the nineteenth century.

V. George, *Social Security and Society* (1973).

B. B. Gilbert, *The Evolution of National Insurance* (1966).
The indispensable account of the origins of the major Liberal reforms. Excellent annotated bibliography.

R. Gregory, *The Miners and British Politics, 1906–14* (Oxford University Press, 1968).

E. Halévy, *History of the English People in the 19th Century*, volume 5 : *Imperialism and the Rise of Labour*, volume 6 : *The Rule of Democracy, 1905–14* (1961 ed.). (Originally published in French in 1932).
Together these form the best comprehensive account of the period. There is much still to be learnt from both volumes.

J. F. Harris, *Unemployment and Politics, 1886–1914* (Oxford University Press, 1972).
First-class account of the development of official policy on unemployment. Contains very full bibliography.

L. T. Hobhouse, *Liberalism* (1911).

E. J. Hobshawm, *Labouring Men* (1964).
Contains a review of MacBriar (1962) which tries to account for the emergence of Fabian socialism, and its failure to influence the Liberals decisively.

R. Jenkins, *Asquith* (1964).
Well received biography which does not do justice to Asquith's taxation policy or social reform.

H. Levy, *National Health Insurance* (Cambridge University Press, 1944).
Subtitled 'a critical study'.

T. Lummis, 'Charles Booth, Moralist or Social Scientist?', *Economic History Review*, 24 (1971).
Debate with J. Brown (1968, 1971) on Booth's moral judgements.

H. M. Lynd, *England in the 1880s: Towards a Social Basis for Freedom* (Oxford University Press, 1945).

A. M. MacBriar, *Fabian Socialism and English Politics, 1884–1918* (Cambridge University Press, 1962).
Shows why the Fabian influence was less than Fabians claimed.

O. R. McGregor, 'Social Research and Social Policy in the 19th Century', *British Journal of Sociology*, 8 (1957).
Puts the late nineteenth-century poverty studies into a wider context.

R. I. McKibbin, 'J. R. MacDonald and the Problem of the Independence of the Labour Party, 1910–14', *Journal of Modern History*, 42 (1970).

R. MacLeod, 'The Frustration of State Medicine, 1880–1899', *Medical History*, 11 (1967).

R. MacLeod, *Treasury Control and Social Administration* (1968).

T. H. Marshall, *Sociology at the Crossroads* (1963).
Contains the important essay 'Citizenship and Social Class' of 1950.

T. H. Marshall, *Social Policy* (1965).
Brief, but still valuable.

E. W. Martin (ed.), *Comparative Development in Social Welfare* (1972).
Mainly on the early nineteenth century, but has introduction by A. Briggs which continues the analysis of research begun in Briggs (1961*b*).

A. Marwick, 'The Labour Party and the Welfare State in Britain 1900–48', *American Historical Review*, 73 (1967).
Argues, *inter alia*, that the Labour Party had a positive policy on social reform before 1914.

C. F. G. Masterman, *The Condition of England* (1909).
Analysis of English society by one of the younger 'New Liberals'.

H. C. G. Matthew, *The Liberal Imperialists* (Oxford University Press, 1973).
Concentrates on the views of the small group around Rosebery between 1895 and 1905.

L. G. Chiozza Money, *Riches and Poverty* (1905).
An analysis of the distribution of wealth and income. Influential, though criticised by the Treasury.

K. O. Morgan, *The Age of Lloyd George* (1971).
Commentary and documents.

C. L. Mowat, 'The Approach to the Welfare State in Great Britain', *American Historical Review*, 58 (1952–3).

C. L. Mowat, *The Charity Organisation Society, 1869–1913* (1961).

C. L. Mowat, 'Social Legislation in Britain and the United States in the Early Twentieth Century : a Problem in the History of Ideas', in *Historical Studies*, vii (1969).

S. Nowell-Smith (ed.), *Edwardian England, 1900–1914* (1964).
Series of essays including one by A. Briggs on the political scene, and one by A. J. Taylor on the economy.

A. T. Peacock and J. V. Wiseman, *The Growth of Public Expenditure in the United Kingdom* (2nd ed., 1967).
A statistical account.

H. M. Pelling, *Popular Politics and Society in Late Victorian Britain* (1969).
Chapter 1 argues that the working class, on the whole, opposed the welfare reforms.

M. Petter, 'The Progressive Alliance', *History*, 58 (1973).
Criticises the new orthodoxy which tends to link the Labour and Liberal Parties in a progressive alliance before 1914.

E. H. Phelps Brown, *The Growth of British Industrial Relations* (1959).
Excellent blend of economics and history. Contains much more than industrial relations as conventionally defined.

R. Pinker, *Social Theory and Social Policy* (1971).

F. L. Pryor, *Public Expenditure in Communist and Capitalist Nations* (1968).
A survey by an economist, which examines some historical hypotheses about the growth of welfare services. Excellent bibliography.

D. Read, *Edwardian England* (1972).
Has one chapter on the 'Social Service State'.

G. Riddell, *More Pages From My Diary, 1908–14* (1934).
Useful for the origins of national insurance.

G. V. Rimlinger, 'Welfare Policy and Economic Development : a Comparative Historical Perspective', *Journal of Economic History*, 26 (1966).

G. V. Rimlinger, *Welfare Policy and Industrialisation in Europe, America and Russia* (New York, 1971).
A comparative study of considerable merit. Many of his ideas can be developed in the light of recent work.

B. C. Roberts, *The Trades Union Congress* (1958).

M. E. Rose, *The English Poor Law, 1780–1930* (Newton Abbot, (1971).
Commentary and documents.

M. E. Rose, *The Relief of Poverty, 1834–1914* (1972).

H. Roseveare, *The Treasury* (1969).
An excellent account covering 1066 to 1960s. Chapters 6 and 7 are relevant to the origins of the reforms.

P. Rowland, *The Last Liberal Governments: the Promised Land, 1905–10* (1968).

A. K. Russell, *Liberal Landslide* (Newton Abbot, 1973).
An analysis of the 1906 election results.

H. Samuel, *Liberalism: Its Principles and Proposals* (1902).
An early statement of the changes in Liberalism.

D. F. Schloss, *Insurance Against Unemployment* (1909).
A survey of foreign schemes considered by the Liberals.

K. de Schweinitz, *England's Road to Social Security* (University of Pennsylvania, 1943).
Brief but useful general account.

G. R. Searle, *The Quest for National Efficiency* (Oxford, 1971).
A study in ideas and politics, which does not examine social imperialism.

B. Semmel, *Imperialism and Social Reform* (1960).
Develops Halévy's link between imperialism and social reform, but does not make explicit the links with the Liberal reforms.

F. Shehab, *Progressive Taxation* (Oxford University Press, 1953).

T. S. and M. B. Simey, *Charles Booth* (Oxford University Press, (1960).

R. V. Sires, 'The Beginning of British Legislation for Old Age Pensions', *Journal of Economic History*, 14 (1954).
To be read in conjunction with Gilbert (1966) and Treble (1970).

G. Slater, *Poverty and the State* (1930).
Wide-ranging early account.

G. Stedman Jones, *Outcast London* (Oxford University Press, 1971).

S. G. Tallents, *Man and Boy* (1943).
Contains some information on the early stages of national insurance.

E. P. Thompson and E. Yeo, *The Unknown Mayhew* (1971).

P. Thompson, *Socialists, Liberals and Labour* (1967).
Argues that the Liberal Party in London was being overtaken by Labour.

R. M. Titmuss, *Essays on the Welfare State* (1963).

P. Townsend (ed.), *The Concept of Poverty* (1970).

J. H. Treble, 'The Attitude of the Friendly Societies Towards the Movement in Great Britain for State Pensions, 1878–1908', *International Review of Social History*, 15 (1970).

B. Webb, *My Apprenticeship* (1926).

B. Webb, *Our Partnership*, ed. B. Drake and M. Cole (1948).
The Webbs were closely involved in the debate on social reform, but these two sources of information on their activities have to be used with care.

G. Williams, *The State and the Standard of Living* (1936).

D. Winch, *Economics and Policy* (1972 ed.).
A first-class account of the interrelationships of economic thought and policy, based on secondary sources.

C. Woodard, 'Reality and Social Reform : the Transition from *Laissez-faire* to the Welfare State', *Yale Law Journal*, 72 (1962).

K. Woodroofe, *From Charity to Social Work* (1962).
Deals with Britain and the United States.

ADDENDUM FOR THE REVISED EDITION, 1983

Since the first edition of this work was completed, research on the origins of the Liberal Reforms has continued unabated. The extent and the proximate causes of urban poverty have been carefully delineated by J. H. Treble, while changing ideas and attitudes regarding poverty and potential remedies are discussed in Freeden, Garraty (in a very wide context), Hennock, Pinker, Thane (1978) and MacKenzie's edition of the Webbs' correspondence. Hennock's challenging article invites consideration as to whether periods of maximum public interest in questions of poverty necessarily coincide with innovations in theoretical understanding or legislation.

Comparative studies of the origins of modern welfare legislation, which it was hoped might illuminate more clearly the distinctive features of the Liberal Reforms, have not quite borne out the optimism expressed in the first edition. These have developed in four main ways. There have been one or two quite ambitious attempts at building and testing comprehensive, quantitative models by Flora and Heidenheimer and by Collier and Messick. The quantitative precision of these models often disguises their conceptual fuzziness. Some less methodologically adventurous comparative studies contain shrewd historical insights, including Kaim-Caudle and the collection edited by Mommsen. A second approach has been the continuing search for alternative frameworks for analysis by Rimlinger, Hall *et al.*, Higgins, Madison, Carrier and Kendall, Gough and Rein (in Henderson). These could be judged by the fruitfulness of the results or by their stimulation to thought and further research, and it would be fair to say that it is in the latter respects that they are valuable so far. Then there are country-by-country studies of social policy, of which the collection by Köhler and Zacher is representative. It provides a useful introduction to the secondary literature on social insurance. Finally, there are some interesting studies of the transfer of ideas and institutions between societies (Rickard, Mommsen and Sutcliffe) which have begun to demonstrate more clearly what British legislation owed to foreign models and where it differed. Thane's textbook (1982) tries to tackle this problem by devoting a separate chapter to foreign practice and has some useful suggestions for further research.

At apparently the other extreme, studies of 'localities' and the local impact of policies, prior to and after the reforms, have grown in number and quality. Such work has focused on the Poor Law (Digby, Vorspan) and on debates about the 'local state', a concept whose significance has been re-emphasised by Yeo and the contributors to Melling (ed., 1980).

The contribution of various social groups in Britain to the origins of social legislation has been analysed by several writers. Melling and Hay have examined the role of employers, Bebbington has discussed

Nonconformists, while Dutton has outlined the different strands of Unionist policy, concluding that social reform was a very low priority indeed. The influence of civil servants is carefully and interestingly explained by Davidson and Lowe in Mommsen, by Whiteside and by Harris in her biography of Beveridge. The response of labour is touched on in many works, including Howkins, but still awaits Thane's paper, which may well appear before this edition is in print. Meanwhile, her discussion of the Poor Law's treatment of women is complemented by Crowther's contribution to Thane (1978) and her book on the workhouse system. The politics of legislation is covered by Gilbert, Grigg and Murray, while Ramsden is the best modern introduction to conservatism. Offer has restored land to a central place in the debates of the period, thus throwing much indirect, though illuminating, light on the welfare reforms. The economic background is finely portrayed by Gourvish in Chapter 1 of O'Day, which otherwise eschews detailed treatment of the Liberal welfare reforms.

The detailed study of individual pieces of legislation continues, however, and can be found in Simmons' and Rickard's work on mental illness and sweating respectively. Both place the laws studied firmly in context. J. Walley's idiosyncratic account of twentieth-century social policy includes information which is not to be found elsewhere. Some alternative theoretical approaches have been explored. Social control as an explanation for legislation has been discussed by Brown and Hay in Thane (ed., 1978) and by Higgins, but has been attacked from the perspective of structural linguistics by Williams. This inconoclastic book repays careful attention. Finally, documentary collections with material bearing on the Liberal Reforms include Evans, Hay (ed., 1978) and Thane (1982).

D. W. Bebbington, *The Non-Conformist Conscience: Chapel and Politics, 1870–1914* (1982).

J. Carrier and I. Kendall, 'The Development of Welfare States: The Production of Plausible Accounts', *Journal of Social Policy*, 6 (1977).

D. Collier and R. Messick, 'Prerequisites versus Diffusion: Testing Alternative Explanations of Social Security Adoption', *American Political Science Review*, 69 (1975).

S. Collini, *Liberalism and Sociology: L. T. Hobhouse and Political Argument in England, 1880–1914* (Cambridge, 1979).

M. A. Crowther, *The Workhouse System, 1834–1929* (1981).

A. Digby, *Pauper Palaces* (1978).

A. Digby, *The New Poor Law in Nineteenth Century England and Wales*, Historical Association Pamphlet, General Series, 104 (1982).

D. J. Dutton, 'The Unionist Party and Social Policy, 1906–1914', *Historical Journal*, 24 (1981).

E. J. Evans, *Social Policy, 1830–1914* (1978).

P. Flora and A. J. Heidenheimer, *The Development of Welfare States in Europe and America* (New Brunswick, New Jersey, 1981).

D. Fraser (ed.), *The New Poor Law in the Nineteenth Century* (1976).

D. Fraser, *The Evolution of the British Welfare State*, 2nd edn (1983).

M. Freeden, *The New Liberalism: An Ideology of Social Reform* (Oxford, 1978).

J. A. Garraty, *Unemployment in History: Economic Thought and Public Policy* (New York, 1978).

E. Gauldie, *Cruel Habitations* (1974).

B. B. Gilbert, 'David Lloyd George, Land, the Budget and Social Reform', *American Historical Review*, 81 (1976).

I. Gough, *The Political Economy of the Welfare State* (1979).

J. Grigg, *Lloyd George: The People's Champion, 1902–1911* (1978).

P. Hall, H. Land, R. Parker and A. Webb, *Change, Choice and Conflict in Social Policy* (1975).

J. F. Harris, *William Beveridge: A Biography* (Oxford, 1977).

J. R. Hay, 'Government Policy toward Labour in Britain, 1900–1914', *Scottish Labour History Journal*, 10 (1976).

J. R. Hay, 'Employers and Social Policy in Britain: The Evolution of Welfare Legislation, 1905–1914', *Social History*, 4 (1977).

J. R. Hay (ed.), *The Development of the British Welfare State, 1880–1975* (1978).

J. R. Hay, 'The Comparative Study of the Development of Social Welfare Policy', *Australian Historical Association Bulletin*, 17 (1978).

R. F. Henderson (ed.), *The Welfare Stakes* (Melbourne, 1981).

E. P. Hennock, 'Poverty and Social Theory in England: The Experience of the 1880s', *Social History*, 1 (1976).

J. Higgins, 'Social Control Theories of Social Policy', *Journal of Social Policy*, 9 (1980).

J. Higgins, *States of Welfare: Comparative Analysis of Social Policy* (1981).

A. Howkins, 'Edwardian Liberalism and Industrial Unrest: A Class View of the Decline of Liberalism', *History Workshop Journal*, 4 (1977).

P. Joyce, *Work, Society and Politics: The Culture of the Factory in Later Victorian England* (Sussex, 1980).

P. R. Kaim-Caudle, *Comparative Social Policy and Social Security* (1973).

P. A. Köhler and H. F. Zacher (eds), *The Evolution of Social Insurance, 1881–1981* (1982).

J. Lewis, 'Social History of Social Policy', *Journal of Social Policy*, 9 (1980).

B. Q. Madison, *The Meaning of Social Policy: The Comparative Dimension in Social Welfare* (1980).

J. Melling, 'Non-Commissioned Officers: British Employers and their Supervisory Workers, 1880–1920', *Social History*, 5, (1980).

J. Melling (ed.), *Housing, Social Policy and the State* (1980).

J. Melling, 'Employers, Industrial Housing and the Evolution of Company Welfare Policies in Britain's Heavy Industry: West Scotland, 1870–1920', *International Review of Social History*, 26 (1981).

R. Mishra, *Society and Social Policy: Theoretical Perspectives on Welfare* (1977).

W. J. Mommsen (ed.), *The Emergence of the Welfare State in Britain and Germany, 1850–1950* (1981).

B. K. Murray, *The People's Budget, 1909–10: Lloyd George and Liberal Politics* (Oxford, 1981).

A. O'Day, *The Edwardian Age: Conflict and Stability, 1900–1914* (1979).

A. Offer, *Property and Politics, 1870–1914: Landownership, Law, Ideology and Urban Development in England* (Cambridge,

1981).

R. A. Pinker, *The Idea of Welfare* (1979).

J. Ramsden, *The Age of Balfour and Baldwin, 1902–1940* (1978).

J. Rickard, 'The Anti-Sweating Movement in Britain and Victoria: The Politics of Empire and Social Reform', *Historical Studies*, 18 (University of Melbourne, 1978–9).

G. V. Rimlinger, 'Historical Analysis of National Welfare Systems', in R. L. Ransom *et al.* (eds), *Explorations in the New Economic History* (New York, 1982).

W. A. Robson, *Welfare State and Welfare Society: Illusion and Reality* (1976).

J. Roe (ed.), *Social Policy in Australia* (Sydney, 1976).

R. J. Scally, *The Origins of the Lloyd George Coalition: The Politics of Social Imperialism, 1900–1918* (1975).

G. R. Searle, *Eugenics and Politics in Britain, 1900–1914* (Leyden, 1976).

H. G. Simmons, 'Explaining Social Policy: The English Mental Deficiency Act of 1913', *Journal of Social History*, 11 (1978).

A. Sutcliffe, *Towards the Planned City* (Oxford, 1981).

P. Thane (ed.), *The Origins of British Social Policy* (1978).

P. Thane, 'Women and the Poor Law in Victorian and Edwardian Britain', *History Workshop Journal*, 6 (1978).

P. Thane, *The Foundation of the Welfare State* (1982).

J. H. Treble, *Urban Poverty in Britain, 1830–1914* (1979).

J. Walley, *Social Security: Another British Failure?* (1972).

N. Mackenzie (ed.), Sidney and Beatrice Webb, *Letters*, 3 Volumes (1978).

R. Vorspan, 'Vagrancy and the New Poor Law in Late Victorian and Edwardian England', *English Historical Review*, 92 (1977).

P. Weiler, *The New Liberalism: Liberal Social Theory in Great Britain, 1889–1914* (New York, 1982).

N. Whiteside, 'Welfare Insurance and Casual Labour: A Study of Administrative Intervention in Industrial Employment, 1906–1926', *Economic History Review*, 32 (1979).

K. Williams, *From Pauperism to Poverty* (1981).

H. R. Winkler (ed.), *Twentieth Century Britain: National Power and Social Welfare* (New York, 1976).

S. Yeo, 'Working-Class Association, Private Capital, Welfare and the State in the late Nineteenth and Twentieth Centuries', in N. Parry, M. Rustin and C. Satyamurti (eds), *Social Work, Welfare and the State* (1979).

Keynes, J. M. 17

labour colonies 48–9
labour exchanges 50–1, 61
Labour Party 22, 26–7, 29,
    43–4, 52, 55, 59–61;
    Labour government
    (1945–51) 20; Labour
    M.P.s 46, 50, 61
laissez-faire 11
Lancashire 22; cotton famine
    47
Lansbury, George 49
Liberal Party 11, 22, 26,
    32–3, 35, 43–4, 46, 49,
    52–3; Liberal Imperialists
    30; Liberal M.P.s 46;
    New Liberalism 35, 51,
    53
Llewellyn Smith, Sir Hubert
    39
Lloyd George, D. 15–16, 20,
    32, 35, 50–1, 53, 56–61
local authorities 17, 26, 38,
    40–1, 43–4, 48–9, 52
Local Government Board 23,
    39–40, 42, 49, 54; Medical
    Department 23, 54
London 22, 48
Long, Walter 49

MacDonagh, O. 22
MacDonald, Ramsay 53
Marshall, A., 34, 37, 42, 44,
    47, 57
Marxism 37
Marxist analysis of welfare
    18–19, 30
Masterman, C. F. G. 35
Mayhew, H. 33

Mill, J. S. 35
miners 53
minimum wages 11, 52–3
Morant, Sir Robert 44
Morley, John 37

National Committee of
    Organised Labour on Old
    Age Pensions 15, 38, 46
national efficiency 17, 30–4,
    43–5, 46–7, 54, 61
national insurance 11–12, 32,
    38, 41, 45, 47–52, 54–7,
    59–61, 63; National Insur-
    ance Bill 52, 63; insurance
    principle 40, 51
nationalisation 53
New Liberalism 35, 51, 53.
    See also Liberal Party
New Zealand 15, 46
Newman, Sir George 44

old age pensions 11–12, 19,
    27, 32–4, 38, 41, 45–7, 59

Pigou, A. C. 34
Playfair, Sir Lyon 31
political reasons for the growth
    of welfare 18, 20, 25–9,
    43–4, 47–53
Poor Law 26–7, 34, 38, 41–2,
    48, 50, 54–5, 57; Poor Law
    Guardians 42–3, 49. See
    also Royal Commission on
    the Poor Laws
pressure groups 15, 38, 45–6,
    55–7
psephology 22
public health 54, 56
public works 52